LOTUS 98T

**Includes all Lotus-Renault F1 cars,
1983 to 1986 (93T, 94T, 95T, 97T & 98T)**

COVER CUTAWAY: **Lotus 98T.** *(Roy Scorer)*

First published in April 2016

A catalogue record for this book is available
from the British Library.

ISBN 978 0 85733 777 1

Library of Congress control no. 2015944341

Design and layout by James Robertson

Published by Haynes Publishing,
Sparkford, Yeovil,
Somerset BA22 7JJ, UK.
Tel: 01963 440635
Int. tel: +44 1963 440635
Website: www.haynes.co.uk

Haynes North America Inc.,
861 Lawrence Drive, Newbury Park,
California 91320, USA.

Printed in the USA by
Odcombe Press LP,
1299 Bridgestone Parkway,
La Vergne, TN 37086.

LOTUS 98T

Includes all Lotus-Renault F1 cars, 1983 to 1986 (93T, 94T, 95T, 97T & 98T)

Owners' Workshop Manual

An insight into the design, engineering, maintenance and operation of the fastest, most powerful Lotus F1 cars ever raced

Stephen Slater

Contents

Introduction

In many respects the Lotus-Renault 97T and 98T marked a turning point in Formula 1 history. They were the last cars to carry the iconic black and gold John Player Special livery and they also represented the end of Renault's opening chapter in Formula 1 with the revolutionary turbocharged engines that redefined the sight and sound of the sport. They remain the fastest Lotus cars ever built.

These cars also embraced the cutting edge of a fast-changing world of technologies outside of motor racing. When the first Lotus-Renault cars took to the track, electronic data management was almost unheard of, yet by the end of the 1986 season Team Lotus was pioneering the use of portable computers and data loggers, and even transmitting data back from the moving cars to the pits and the team headquarters. The cars broke new ground in advancing the use of carbon-composite construction and crash survival safety structures, their carbonfibre brakes were a direct evolution from those developed for Concorde, and their engines were among the first to feature full electronic management and computer-controlled fuel injection.

The Lotus 97T and 98T pushed both the rulebook and technologies of the time to their absolute limits, creating the most powerful Formula 1 cars ever. Subsequent years would see Formula 1 cars emasculated by power restriction and then, for over 25 years, the outlawing of turbocharging. Those 1985 and 1986 seasons brought no-holds-barred battles between the JPS Lotuses and their McLaren, Williams, Ferrari and Brabham rivals, in the last era of Formula 1 in which horsepower was king.

OPPOSITE Ayrton Senna's legendary focus and early-race aggression was part of a deliberate strategy. *(John Townsend, F1 Pictures)*

ACKNOWLEDGEMENTS

Just as with running a JPS Lotus-Renault, producing a book of this nature requires the input of a range of talented individuals. Prime among them is Patrick Morgan, the owner of the last car to be built, Lotus 98T chassis 04. Not only did Patrick allow us to photograph his car under rebuild, he and fellow DT Performance engineer Mark Robinson took valuable time out from their highly esteemed race car restoration business to transport the car to studios for photography and to share their encyclopaedic knowledge.

Likewise, special thanks are in order to Clive Chapman (son of Lotus founder Colin) and his small, tight-knit team at Classic Team Lotus in Norfolk. Clive, race team manager Chris Dinnage and team co-ordinator Sapphire Nichols have provided invaluable assistance both in terms of enabling access to Classic Team Lotus's extensive archives and, in Chris's case, providing me with fascinating insight into being a part of Team Lotus at the time of the 97T and 98T. To Clive I owe additional thanks for bringing his legendary attention to detail to play on the page proofs. Thank you for righting my many wrongs!

I also owe a debt of gratitude to Andrew Marriott, at the time a director of CSS Promotions, for his insight into the JPS sponsorship activities and his first-hand observations of Senna's recruitment to the team. As it was Andrew who gave me my first full-time job in professional motorsport more than 30 years ago, special thanks are well overdue.

To another period 'insider', former JPS-Lotus press officer Johnny Tipler, I owe thanks for extracts from his interviews with Johnny Dumfries. I also commend his book *Ayrton Senna: The Team Lotus Years* as a great follow-up read. Finally, a big 'thank you' to John Townsend of F1 Pictures, whose contemporary photos of Formula 1 provide the perfect atmospheric backdrop to this record of an unforgettable era.

Stephen Slater
January 2016

Chapter One

The Team Lotus story

For four decades from 1954, Team Lotus exemplified a British spirit of innovation and engineering that led the world. It was the era of the Comet and Concorde, the *Queen Elizabeth 2* and iconic road cars including Lotus's own Elite and Elan models. However, it was on the race track where Colin Chapman's cars truly scored, winning seven Formula 1 Constructors' titles and making World Champions of Jim Clark, Graham Hill, Jochen Rindt, Emerson Fittipaldi and Mario Andretti.

OPPOSITE **The first car to carry the iconic John Player Special colours was the Lotus 72 in 1972. Here Emerson Fittipaldi is seen that year on his way to second place at the French Grand Prix, at Clermont-Ferrand.** *(LAT Photographic)*

Born on 19 May 1928, Lotus founder Colin Chapman studied civil engineering at University College, London (UCL) and looked destined to pursue a career in aviation after joining the University of London Air Squadron and learning to fly. Instead he elected to turn down an officer's commission in the Royal Air Force and returned to UCL, where he graduated in 1949.

Early years

Initially his work was selling aluminium structures for buildings in the early post-war construction boom. However, his attention was increasingly occupied by motorsport, where his Austin Seven-based special called 'Lotus' was notable for a lightweight body made of thin alloy sheets bonded to plywood, making it a front-runner in races and trials organised by the 750 Motor Club.

The success, and prize money, allowed the construction of a second special, called Lotus Mk II. Its Austin Seven chassis was reinforced to allow larger and more highly tuned 1,172cc Ford engines to be fitted. By 1951 the design had evolved into the Lotus Mk III, which pushed the boundaries of the 750MC rulebook to the limit, with the compulsory Austin Seven chassis being augmented by tubular cross-members for added torsional stiffness and a semi-stressed

aluminium two-seater body, which weighed only 65lbs (30kg), providing more rigidity as well as reducing drag.

With the success of the Lotus Mk III in club racing, it became clear to Chapman that there was a market for the cars and key components. On 1 January 1952, in partnership with fellow enthusiasts Michael and Nigel Allen, he established Lotus Engineering behind the Railway Hotel in Hornsey, North London. After inevitable experimentation Chapman came up with a new design that would set the company on the road to success – the Lotus Mk VI.

From the outset Chapman was determined to take advantage of construction techniques used in the aircraft industry and the Mk VI dispensed with the Austin Seven chassis in favour of a lightweight tubular steel 'spaceframe' as used in light aircraft of the time. Weighing just 55lbs (25kg), it was complemented by bolted-on aluminium body panels produced by local panel beaters Williams & Pritchard, who went on to produce many of the Lotus bodies of the next decade.

Chapman rapidly assumed sole control of the business and between 1952 and 1957 over 100 examples of the Mk VI were built and sold, in kit form to avoid the payment of additional purchase taxes. The success of the car was augmented by the arrival in 1953 of Mike

BELOW Colin and Hazel Chapman with the Lotus Mk III. *(SMMT)*

Costin, an engineer with the de Havilland aircraft company, whose aerodynamicist brother Frank subsequently designed a wind-cheating body for the Mk VI, which resulted in the Mk VIII.

A red-letter day came when the cars beat the factory Porsche team in the sports car race preceding the 1954 British Grand Prix at Silverstone, the order book swelling sufficiently to allow Chapman and Mike Costin to give up their day jobs. They began working for Lotus full-time in 1955, the year in which Team Lotus first entered the Le Mans 24 Hours.

The ever-energetic and entrepreneurial Chapman was determined to drive the expansion of both road car and racing car production. On the road car front, a development of the Mk VI – the Mk VII, later simply known as the Lotus Seven – continued to promote the Lotus philosophy of gaining performance through a lightweight and uncomplicated design. Over 2,500 examples of the Seven were produced by Lotus between 1957 and 1972, and derivatives of the design are still in production today.

The Lotus Elite, also introduced in 1957, was a more sophisticated design, replacing the traditional chassis with innovative monocoque construction in glassfibre for the entire load-bearing structure of the aerodynamically styled two-seat coupé. The Elite was powered by a road-tuned version of a lightweight all-alloy engine produced by Coventry Climax, a pre-war car engine maker that was now primarily a producer of industrial power units. The 1,200cc FWE unit was derived from an ultra-light motor designed to power high-pressure water pumps for firefighting, but the FW (for featherweight) derivative engines proved equally successful in motorsport and were a perfect complement to Chapman's lightweight road car philosophies.

In 1962 the Elite's successor, the Lotus Elan, demonstrated both Chapman's design genius and his ability to engage suitable industry partners. Built around an innovative backbone chassis and racing-derived independent suspension, the glassfibre-bodied Elan was powered by a derivative of Ford's 'Kent' 1,500cc engine, which powered mainstream models such as the best-selling Cortina. To boost performance, Chapman commissioned former BRM engineer Harry Mundy to devise a new twin-overhead camshaft cylinder head.

Chapman subsequently sold design rights in this engine to Ford, who named it the 'Lotus-Ford Twin Cam', while future evolutions of the engine led to the creation of the engine builder Cosworth, founded by former Lotus employees Keith Duckworth and Mike Costin. For the next two decades Lotus, Ford and Cosworth were set to be inextricably linked.

The birth of Team Lotus

As early as 1954, with the formation of Team Lotus as a separate company, Colin Chapman formally separated Lotus racing activities from its road car and engineering operations. It rapidly built on the success achieved by its Lotus Mk VI and Mk VIII models in both domestic and international sports car racing, boosted still further by the introduction in 1956 of the Lotus Eleven. Styled by Frank Costin, this model featured a low-slung, all-enveloping aerodynamic body, with the Coventry Climax engine canted over by 45 degrees to lower the centre of gravity as well as the bonnet line.

With over 250 examples built, the Lotus Eleven became one of the most successful light racing sports cars of the 1950s. The customer race cars were led by the Team Lotus entries, sometimes driven by Chapman himself, but increasingly he

BELOW The Lotus 11 combined Colin Chapman's spaceframe chassis with Mike Costin's aerodynamic styling to create an international race winner.
(Ian Wagstaff)

ABOVE The Lotus 12, Colin Chapman's first grand prix car, was powered by a Coventry Climax engine. (Author)

BELOW With side panels removed for cooling, Stirling Moss takes the Rob Walker Lotus 18 to the marque's first grand prix victory, at Monaco in 1960. (Lotus)

delegated the responsibility to Cumbrian Cliff Allison and Southampton businessman and Formula 3 racer Reg Bicknell, who effectively became the first Team Lotus drivers.

In addition to success in sports car racing, the Lotus Eleven, usually powered by Coventry Climax's 1,100cc FWA engine but later the larger FWB, also proved to be surprisingly competitive in Formula 2 races for single-seat 1½-litre cars. It was logical, therefore, for Chapman to produce his first purpose-designed single-seater in 1957. The Lotus 12 featured innovations such as a rear-mounted, five-speed, sequential-shift transaxle to reduce transmission height and improve weight distribution, and a new design of rear suspension subsequently

known as the 'Chapman strut', which combined a MacPherson strut coil-spring-over-damper unit with the driveshaft acting as a lower suspension link to reduce weight. This lightweight car's ability to run a whole race on just a single set of tyres also allowed the first use in motor racing of lightweight, cast-magnesium 'wobbly web' wheels, using a multi-bolt fastening instead of a 'knock-on' central shaft and spinner.

Lotus 12s raced in Formula 1 as well as Formula 2 after Coventry Climax successively introduced 2-litre and 2½-litre engines. Despite a shoestring budget, the efforts of drivers Cliff Allison and Graham Hill (elevated from his position as a Team Lotus mechanic) allowed the Lotus 12 to achieve encouraging results, including sixth place on the car's début in the 1957 Monaco Grand Prix. However, the front-engined Lotus 12 and its successor, the Lotus 16, were ultimately outclassed by the mid-engined Coopers, which had superior slow-speed traction.

Formula 1 success

In late 1959 Chapman came up with his answer – the Lotus 18. In addition to having its engine behind the driver, a further innovation was its reclined seating position, which reduced frontal area and lowered the centre of gravity. The double wishbone front suspension was also complemented by a reversal of the design of the 'Chapman strut' rear suspension, with the assembly being inverted to allow the driveshaft to act as the suspension's upper link.

The Lotus 18's suspension configuration significantly reduced weight transfer and body roll, providing cornering speeds higher than had ever been seen in grand prix racing. Despite a power deficit to some of the opposition from the now-venerable Climax FPF engine, the car was a winner. Lotus's first World Championship race victory came at Monaco in May 1960, with Stirling Moss taking the chequered flag in a Lotus 18 operated by privateer team owner Rob Walker.

Team Lotus's first Formula 1 victory of its own came with a Lotus 21, when Innes Ireland won the 1961 United States Grand Prix. Equally auspiciously, Ireland was joined in the team at

RIGHT This line-up of original Team Lotus mechanics includes Bob Dance (third from left), who was set to become chief mechanic in the Senna era. *(Classic Team Lotus)*

CENTRE Maestro at work. Jim Clark at the wheel of the Lotus-Climax 25 during 1963, the year in which he won his, and Team Lotus's, first Formula 1 World Championship. *(Lotus)*

that time by a fast-rising young Scot called Jim Clark, whose name would become synonymous with the team.

Clark graduated to Team Lotus after proving a front-runner in the British Formula Junior Championship in a Lotus. His versatile style also allowed him to win in seemingly effortless style in Lotus Elan sports cars and Lotus Cortina racing saloons, but it was at the wheel of Chapman's Formula 1 cars that he showed his true forte.

Clark's first grand prix victory for Team Lotus came in 1962 at Spa-Francorchamps, Belgium, when he fought his way from 12th place on the grid to beat pole-sitter Graham Hill, now driving for BRM, to the chequered flag. It was the beginning of six successive wins for Clark at the Ardennes track and, additionally, the first win for the new Lotus 25, which again showed Chapman's adoption of aircraft engineering techniques, with the use of the 'ACBC Twin Boom' chassis of semi-monocoque design. Clark also won the British Grand Prix at Aintree and the United States Grand Prix at Watkins Glen to finish second in the 1962 World Championship.

In 1963 Clark and the Lotus 25 dominated, winning seven out of the ten races to give Clark his first Drivers' World Championship and Team Lotus its first Constructors' title. In addition, Colin Chapman sealed a deal with Ford to develop a car, the Lotus 29, for the Indianapolis 500, where Clark led 28 of the 200 laps to finish in second place behind veteran Parnelli Jones and take Rookie of the Year honours.

RIGHT The Lotus Ford twin-cam engine powered both the Elan and the Lotus Cortina; here Jim Clark heads for victory at Brand Hatch. *(Ford)*

RIGHT The Hare and the Tortoise. Jim Clark poses in an Elan for an unconventional 1965 press shot. (Lotus)

BELOW Jim Clark in his Lotus 33 at Copse Corner, Silverstone, on his way to winning the British Grand Prix in 1965, the year he became World Champion for the second time. (Lotus)

BELOW RIGHT The legendary Cosworth DFV engine first appeared in 1967, in the Lotus 49, winning on its début at the Dutch Grand Prix.
(Ian Wagstaff)

In comparison, 1964 was a relatively fallow year with Clark narrowly conceding the World Championship crown to John Surtees, but in 1965 Team Lotus was back on form. In addition to victories in Tasman series, Formula 2 and touring car racing, six wins in his Climax-powered Lotus 33 gave Clark his second Drivers' World Championship and Lotus its second Constructors' title. The Scot also took the Ford-engined Lotus 38 to Victory Lane at Indianapolis, the first mid-engined car to win the American classic and the first fully stressed monocoque design.

A change in Formula 1 regulations for the 1966 season increased engine capacity to a maximum of 3 litres and led to Chapman striking a deal to use BRM's new P75 H16-cylinder engine. While the new engine looked good on paper, it is said that Team Lotus engineers sensed trouble when the first example arrived at Lotus's headquarters in Hethel, Norfolk and required four men to lift it from the truck. As well as being overweight, the engine proved to be unreliable and unable to produce the promised power. In 1966 Clark did not win until the end of the season, in the United States Grand Prix at Watkins Glen, and history records this as the only ever race win for the BRM H-16 engine.

The 1967 season was a very different story as an all-new car and engine combination made its appearance. The Lotus 49 was powered by an engine that had come about as a result of Chapman's road-car relationships with Ford and with the Northamptonshire firm of Cosworth, which had been created by former Lotus

employees Mike Costin and Keith Duckworth. Cosworth had already successfully developed the BDA (for Belt-Driven Anglia) racing derivative of the Ford Kent engine used in Cortina and Anglia road cars. Chapman famously persuaded Ford's public affairs director Walter Hayes to invest £100,000 so that Cosworth could develop an all-alloy, four-valve version of the BDA engine (the FVA, for 'Four-Valve Anglia') and a 3-litre V8 for Formula 1 use (the DFV, for 'Double Four-Valve'). With the benefit of hindsight, Ford's investment was outstandingly successful. The Ford-Cosworth DFV went on to win 158 grands prix between 1967 and 1983, a significant proportion of them in Lotus cars.

Team Lotus had exclusive use of the DFV engine for the 1967 season. After winning on the Lotus 49's début in the Dutch Grand Prix at Zandvoort, Clark went on to score three more victories and finished second in the World Championship. There were many teething troubles, however, and three retirements potentially cost Clark the title. Team-mate Graham Hill fared even worse as he was forced to retire from seven of the nine races he contested in the Lotus that year.

The opening race of the 1968 season saw Clark and Hill score a 1–2 victory in South Africa, but the sport was rocked by tragedy when, on 7 April 1968, Clark was killed in a Formula 2 race at Hockenheim in Germany. The accident shook Team Lotus to its core, but it was a sign of the strength of the team and the capability of the Lotus-Ford package that Graham Hill scored three more victories

that season on his way to his second World Champion's crown, having won his first with BRM in 1962.

The 1968 season was to prove pivotal in other ways too. Lotus was a pioneer in the use of aerofoils to generate aerodynamic downforce to increase tyre grip, with the car initially using inverted wing sections mounted on struts attached to the front and rear suspension, but after a series of structural failures these were banned, with 'wings' then being incorporated into the nosecone and rear bodywork.

An equally fundamental change came with the cars' livery. When the Team Lotus cars appeared at the Spanish Grand Prix in May 1968, they shocked the establishment by carrying not the traditional British Racing Green, the national colour for UK teams

in international motorsport, but a red and gold livery representing the John Player Gold Leaf cigarette brand, as part of a commercial sponsorship deal with the Imperial Tobacco Group. Once again, Chapman's spirit of innovation had created a deal that represented a totally new initiative for Formula 1 teams, which until then had usually only struck sponsorship deals 'in kind' with the motor industry and technical suppliers. The creation of 'Gold Leaf Team Lotus' opened the door to other tobacco manufacturers such as Embassy, Marlboro and Gitanes, as well as other sponsors such as cosmetics maker Yardley, as the Gold Leaf livery gained

international exposure on the Lotus 49 and Lotus 72 cars between 1968 and 1971.

The innovative chisel-nosed, wedge-shaped Lotus 72, widely considered one of the most attractive Formula 1 cars ever built, arrived in 1970. The car pushed the limits of contemporary technology with rising-rate torsion bar suspension, side-mounted radiators for its Cosworth DFV engine and inboard front brakes to optimise aerodynamic performance, allowing Jochen Rindt to win four successive mid-season races and lead the championship, before a crash in practice for the Italian Grand Prix claimed his life. At the end of the season, Rindt became Formula 1's first and only posthumous World Champion.

Another new chapter began in 1971. Rindt's replacement, Emerson Fittipaldi, initially struggled with an updated version of the 72, but then went on to win five races and claim the 1972 World Championship. The revised car also featured a brand new and highly distinctive black and gold livery that reflected a new cigarette brand from Imperial Tobacco. In the eyes of the marketing people at least, the car was no longer a Lotus and instead was a 'John Player Special'. A new era in motorsport had begun.

JPS – the Cosworth years

The creation of the now iconic black and gold John Player Special (JPS) livery met with emphatic disapproval from some of the establishment. Denis Jenkinson, revered continental correspondent of *Motor Sport*, refused to attend any events he deemed 'mere sponsor announcements' and never used the team's new title in his reports. For him the cars would always be Lotuses.

John Player's key marketeers, George Hadfield and Noel Stanbury, were astute and experienced in developing their sponsorship message to the wider public. At the end of 1971, after three seasons of Gold Leaf identity, they proposed that Lotus should form a key part of the launch of the new John Player Special brand. At an informal meeting at Hadfield's home, graphic designer Barry Foley, racer of Lotus 7 and Clubmans sports cars as well as the originator of *Autosport*'s 'Catchpole'

cartoon, sketched his thoughts for Team Lotus's new livery, using the JPS packaging style as the basis. (Hadfield's son Simon, incidentally, is today a leading restorer and racer of historic machinery, including classic JPS Lotus cars!) Not only did the team's Lotus 72s carry the new black and gold livery, but so did everything else – team clothing, motorhome, transporters and even Chapman's personal Piper Navajo executive aircraft.

'JPS had the first-ever motorhome to be seen in a Formula 1 paddock,' says Andrew Marriott of CSS Promotions, which handled the JPS publicity operation. 'It was something that Chapman had noted in the USA and he convinced John Player head of sponsorship Peter Dyke to sponsor that as well. We were also the first team to circulate after every practice session and the race a photocopied press bulletin on JPS paper. Before then journalists had to wander around the paddock finding out for themselves.'

The 1971 season had not been a happy one for Gold Leaf Team Lotus, the team having struggled to come to terms with revised tyre specifications, leaving Jackie Stewart and Tyrrell to dominate. The 1972 season and the new JPS era, however, saw the Lotus 72 return to the winner's circle in style. Emerson Fittipaldi won the Spanish, Belgian, British, Austrian and Italian Grands Prix on his way to becoming, at 25, the youngest-ever Formula 1 World Champion.

For 1973 the Lotus 72E was upgraded with the addition of mandatory deformable structures around its monocoque 'tub'. Fittipaldi won

three of the first four races of the season, but thereafter Stewart again dominated and took his third World Championship title. By mid-season the Brazilian was outpaced not only by the Scot but also by his new team-mate, Ronnie Peterson, who drove in flamboyant style to score four late-season victories, finishing third in the Drivers' World Championship just three points behind Fittipaldi, allowing Lotus to claim its fifth Constructors' title.

The JPS sponsorship proved to be an astute investment and the brand became a market leader. As restrictions on tobacco advertising gathered pace, the distinctive livery provided recognition even when use of the brand name and logos was not allowed. Better still for the sponsor, the colours seemed to bond with the fashions of the time and special-edition JPS-liveried road cars, including Lotus Europas and Ford Capris, became sought-after.

Blind alleys

The JPS relationship, however, was to be sorely tested in subsequent years. For 1974, Chapman and Australian designer Ralph Bellamy penned the Lotus 76, which had a smoother aerodynamic profile and was set to be 100lbs (45kg) lighter than its predecessor. Badged for the first time not as a Lotus but as a 'JPS-Ford', the 76 proved to be a complete failure. It suffered a string of mechanical and braking problems and, it turned out, was ultimately no lighter than its predecessor.

Peterson's only wins of the 1974 season in fact came with the now-venerable Lotus

ABOVE Emerson Fittipaldi winning at Montjuïch Park, Spain, in 1973, one of seven grand prix victories for Team Lotus that year with the venerable 72, now in its fourth season. *(Lotus)*

ABOVE **Colin Chapman with his company Piper Navajo, in the sponsor's colours, and his latest road car, the Lotus Esprit S2.** *(Lotus)*

72, which the Swede used to win in Monaco, France and Italy. Victory at Monza was particularly sweet: in one of the closest finishes in grand prix history, Peterson crossed the line just 0.8sec ahead of Fittipaldi, who was now a McLaren driver and was heading for his second World Championship title.

The failure of the Lotus 76 meant that the elderly 72 would have to soldier on into 1975, its sixth season. Unsurprisingly, the year was Team Lotus's least successful since entering grand prix racing in 1960. Peterson's best result was fourth place, in the Monaco Grand Prix, while team-mate Jacky Ickx scored just three championship points before departing at mid-season, leaving relatively inexperienced drivers like Jim Crawford, Brian Henton and John Watson to take turns in the number-two seat.

A new car and new drivers beckoned for 1976, with Mario Andretti and Gunnar Nilsson at the wheel of the 'John Player Special Mk II', otherwise known as the Lotus 77. This Cosworth DFV-powered car was in many ways an interim model, but it featured better aerodynamics than its predecessor and new rocker-arm suspension, which for the first time was fully adjustable to allow fine tuning of camber, castor and ride height for specific tracks. The Lotus 77 was dubbed the 'adjustacar' and its new versatility took

the team some time to accommodate. As James Hunt and Niki Lauda battled for the title in one of the most epic seasons ever, Lotus was a mere supporting player, with Andretti scoring the team's only win in the final race, the waterlogged Japanese Grand Prix.

Chapman, however, was always thinking of his next step and before the end of the 1976 season Team Lotus had already built prototypes of a new car that was set to dominate the 1977 season and change Formula 1 forever.

A year of revolution – 1978
The Lotus 78 introduced the concept of aerodynamic 'ground effect', significantly increasing downforce and cornering speeds. The new Lotus owed its revolutionary performance to wind-tunnel research carried out at Imperial College, London, initially focused on using airflow around the sidepods to generate downforce. During the research, aerodynamicist Peter Wright discovered that the shaped underbody initially developed to feed air through the radiator was itself capable of generating low pressure under the car and hence downforce. This remarkable finding was kept highly secret even after a prototype car was built: the Lotus 78, in fact, was ready to race before the end of the 1976 season, but Chapman insisted that the car be held back until the following year so that rival teams would not be able to develop copycat designs.

The 'John Player Special Mk III' was famously described by Mario Andretti as 'being painted to the road'. While Niki Lauda, driving for Ferrari, netted the Drivers' World Championship with three wins and more consistent points-scoring, the Lotus 78 returned the team to the winner's circle with Andretti scoring four victories, at Long Beach (California), Jarama (Spain), Dijon-Prenois (France) and Monza (Italy), while his Swedish team-mate Gunnar Nilsson scored his first, and only, grand prix win at Zolder (Belgium).

Chapman's 'wing car' leadership continued in 1978, when an even more highly developed variant of the concept appeared. The Lotus 79 had bodywork that extended from the front of the chassis to between the rear wheels, featuring long venturi tunnels to allow the low-pressure area to be created along the whole of

the underside. The new car generated around 30% more downforce than its predecessor, creating such cornering loads that the aluminium honeycomb chassis had to be reinforced continually to handle the stresses.

The Lotus 79 also broke new ground in being the first car to be developed using Computer-Aided Design (CAD) processes and also the first to carry data-logging equipment that could enable computerised analysis of its chassis, braking and engine performance in the pits during a race weekend. This combination of innovations proved devastating to the opposition.

Andretti won five races in the Lotus 79 on his way to the 1978 Drivers' title (in Belgium, Spain, France, Germany and Holland) and Team Lotus claimed the constructors' title thanks to Ronnie Peterson's efforts in achieving four 1–2 finishes as well as victory in the Austrian Grand Prix. However, the season ended in tragedy for the team when the popular Swede succumbed to medical complications after a start-line accident at Monza.

In addition, the 1978 season was to be the last, in the 1970s at least, in which the John Player Special livery was carried. The tobacco company had been steadily reducing its sponsorship commitment for several years and even in their final World Championship-winning

ABOVE **The magnificent Lotus 79 dominated the 1978 season, taking Mario Andretti to the World Championship in a campaign that was marred only by the death of team-mate Ronnie Peterson, following here, after a crash at Monza.** *(John Townsend, F1 Pictures)*

year the cars began to carry increased branding for Olympus Cameras as part of their black and gold livery. At the end of 1978 the JPS sponsorship came to an end.

JPS departure – and return

In 1979, the Lotus 79 and its successor, the 80, appeared in a British Racing Green livery

BELOW **The Lotus 79, here with Ronnie Peterson aboard, pioneered ground-effect aerodynamics, computer-aided design and on-board data logging.** *(John Townsend, F1 Pictures)*

LEFT In 1979 and 1980 Team Lotus cars raced without JPS livery, carrying Martini and Essex Oil branding in the respective years. *(John Townsend, F1 Pictures)*

along with branding from Martini and Tissot watches. In 1980 and early 1981, the Lotus 81 carried the blue, red and chrome colours of Essex Petroleum, a company founded by high-profile, Monaco-based oil trader David Thieme. At its peak the company was said to be making profits of $70 million a year, but the business collapsed in April 1981 and Lotus was left without a sponsor.

CSS, a marketing company that had been established by TV commentators Barrie Gill and Andrew Marriott, was responsible for the JPS and Essex sponsorships, and rapidly reopened negotiations with Imperial Tobacco.

'It was more organic really,' said Marriott. 'They had effectively been outbid by Essex Oil and really wanted to come back. They were marketed in some countries as part of British American Tobacco and we were able to work with them to unlock some additional funding from there.' Just ahead of the Spanish Grand Prix in June 1981 there came a triumphant announcement. The John Player Specials were back!

Driven by Elio de Angelis and Nigel Mansell, the Lotus 87 cars that carried the familiar black and gold livery were regarded merely as stopgaps. A much more radical car, the Lotus 88, had been devised with an ingenious twin-chassis design, one within the other. The inner chassis contained the cockpit structure, engine, transmission and suspension, while the independent outer chassis was designed as an optimal aerodynamic structure, generating huge levels of downforce.

Such was the Lotus 88's likely superiority

CENTRE The twin-chassis Lotus 88 of 1981 was revolutionary but was outlawed by the regulators. *(John Townsend, F1 Pictures)*

LEFT In 1981 the Lotus 87B, a stopgap design after the twin-chassis 88 was banned, pioneered the use of a carbonfibre chassis. *(John Townsend, F1 Pictures)*

RIGHT Ketteringham Hall, the stately headquarters of Team Lotus, is the backdrop for this shot of the Lotus 91 taken at the beginning of the 1982 season. *(John Townsend, F1 Pictures)*

that the Fédération Internationale de l'Automobile (FIA), following a furore created by rival teams, ruled the design inadmissible, forcing Team Lotus to revert to the more conventional 87, which proved to be ill-matched against the dominant Williams FW07. Almost lost amid the politics, the Lotus 88 also featured the first carbon-composite Formula 1 chassis to take to the track – another Team Lotus innovation.

The closing of a chapter – 1982

For 1982 the Lotus 91, a car that marked the end of several eras for the team, carried the JPS livery. This was the last Lotus to be powered by the ubiquitous Ford-Cosworth DFV engine, the last car before 'ground effect' aerodynamics were banned by the regulators, and it marked the last-ever win to be celebrated by Colin Chapman when Elio de Angelis scored a thrilling victory by just 0.05sec over the Williams of Keke Rosberg in the Austrian Grand Prix.

Chapman had realised that the 3-litre V8-powered cars were now being outclassed by the new-generation 1.5-litre V6 turbocharged engines and a deal was struck with Renault to use its power units for the 1983 season. Sadly Chapman was never to see the JPS Lotus-Renault take to the track. On 16 December 1982, at the age of 54, the Lotus founder suffered a fatal heart attack. It was truly the end of an era, but Lotus cars and the JPS livery would race on into perhaps the most exciting times Formula 1 has ever seen – the turbo years.

CENTRE Nigel Mansell in 1982 at the wheel of the Lotus 91. *(John Townsend, F1 Pictures)*

RIGHT The Lotus 91 of 1982 was the last JPS car to use the Cosworth DFV V8 engine, which had served Team Lotus since 1967.
(John Townsend, F1 Pictures)

The late 1970s was a period of some of the most innovative and diverse technologies ever seen in Formula 1. A relatively liberal rulebook enabled such designs as the six-wheel Tyrrells and the advent of 'ground-effect' aerodynamics, but one car maker stood out. At Silverstone on 16 July 1977, Renault Sport introduced totally new technology to Formula 1. Renault's V6 engine featured a startling innovation in Formula 1 – turbocharging – and as a consequence it displaced just 1.5 litres in comparison with the 3-litre normally aspirated opposition.

When the sport's rule-making body, the Commission Sportive Internationale (CSI), introduced the 3-litre formula in 1966, there was a clause that allowed the earlier 1.5-litre engines to continue to be used, boosted by supercharging. As it was unlikely that these mechanically pressurised engines would ever go beyond two bars of boost, or twice atmospheric pressure, what became known as an 'equivalency formula' of 2:1 was deemed fair. A decade and a half later this provided a tempting loophole for the Renault engineers to exploit by turbocharging.

Turbocharging was by no means new technology. The concept was first patented in 1905 by Swiss engineer Dr Alfred Büchi and in the early 1940s exhaust-driven turbochargers were increasingly used in American combat aircraft such as the B-17 Flying Fortress, B-24 Liberator, P-38 Lightning and P-47 Thunderbolt, as well as early post-war airliners such as the Lockheed Constellation. The prime role of aircraft superchargers was to develop relatively low boost pressures to maintain aircraft performance in thinner air at higher altitudes.

The turbocharger is basically a small turbine spun to high revs by exhaust gases, the pressure generated compressing the air flowing into the engine's cylinders. In the 1950s it was realised by companies producing high-performance diesel engines for trucks that the air, when compressed, packs oxygen molecules closer together, meaning that more fuel can be added to the combustion process, increasing efficiency and power.

Initially the technology was deemed more suitable for diesels due to their more robust construction and narrower rev range. However, the combination of readily available small truck-based turbochargers along with improved engine control from electronic ignition and fuel injection made their use in petrol engines increasingly viable. First Chevrolet (with the Corvair Monte Carlo), then BMW, Porsche and SAAB, successfully introduced turbocharged performance engines.

When Renault elected to raise its profile in new overseas markets, Formula 1 was the

BELOW Driven by Jean-Pierre Jabouille, the Renault RS01 made its début in the 1977 British Grand Prix at Silverstone. *(Renault Sport)*

LEFT The RE01 – Renault's original turbocharged power unit. *(Renault Sport)*

natural outlet. The company had a long history in motorsport and in 1968 had acquired the Viry-Châtillon-based Équipe Gordini, which had strong credentials in grand prix and sports car racing. In addition Renault had close links with the Dieppe-based sports car maker Automobiles Alpine, with whom they scored success in rallying and, from 1972, in the Le Mans 24 Hours and Formula 2 with a Gordini-designed 2-litre V6 engine.

In 1976 Renault gave a green light to a dramatic stepping-up of the company's motorsport programme. Alpine and Gordini were amalgamated into a new division called Renault Sport and work began to create both an all-new Formula 1 car and the radical new engine that would be used in both grand prix and sports car racing.

François Castaing, who headed the Renault Sport design team, was the designer of the original Gordini 2-litre V6 engine. While at Alpine, fellow engineer Bernard Dudot, working with another ex-Gordini engineer, Jean-Pierre Boudy, developed a turbocharged version for sports car racing. After reviewing concepts as radical as a normally aspirated W9-cylinder engine, the team settled on the turbocharged V6 engine, maintaining the 86mm bore of the original 2-litre unit, but with reduced stroke to meet the Formula 1 capacity limit.

At the same time André de Cortanze, who had helped design Alpine's Formula 2 and Formula 3 cars, began work on the Renault Sport RS01 chassis, which was initially prepared as a 'proof of concept' as it was thought at this time that Ken Tyrrell would ultimately race the engine in his six-wheel car. Renault's chassis was kept deliberately robust and simple, rather than genuinely competitive. Likewise, the engine was initially built to be strong rather than ultra-light, using a cast-iron cylinder block rather than aluminium.

Another key member of the Renault Sport engineering team was Jean-Pierre Jabouille. In addition to his clear racing talent (he was the 1976 European Formula 2 Champion), Jabouille was a skilled engineer who had developed and built his own racing cars. He was, literally, a driving force behind the Renault Sport efforts.

'We had a small, young team and what we lacked in experience we made up with enthusiasm,' said Bernard Dudot in an interview with *Motor Sport* magazine. 'We started out with very simple mechanical injection and very little turbo response, having to guess at the air/fuel mixture and so on, but gradually we fine-tuned things. Once, we were testing at Jarama and Jean-Pierre said the engine reminded him of a Renault 4 along the straights – then all its power kicked in just as he reached the braking zone. He wasn't sure he'd ever be able to race it.'

The term 'turbo lag' had just been coined – and it was set to become a key characteristic of the cars of the era. Despite the challenges, the Renault RS01 made its race début at the 1977 British Grand Prix and was running in 12th place when, on the 16th lap, an induction manifold split. It was an academic exercise

LEFT The Renault EF1 engine of 1983. *(Renault Sport)*

BELOW The Renault EF4 engine of 1984. *(Renault Sport)*

anyway as the engine's fuel consumption was such the car would have run dry before the chequered flag.

Development work continued apace through the 1977 and 1978 seasons, both in Formula 1 and in endurance sports car racing, where a Renault Sport V6 turbo engine ultimately won the 1978 Le Mans 24 Hours in the Renault Alpine A442 of Didier Pironi and Jean-Pierre Jaussaud. Among the developments was the use of an air and water aftercooler, or intercooler, which allowed the air/fuel charge to be cooled more consistently, allowing better mixture control and fuel consumption.

During the 1977 season the Formula 1 engine was running at around 2.5-bar boost and developing a little over 500bhp. By 1979 the engine, now with twin turbos for better throttle response, was at 3.0-bar boost and rated at over 600bhp, for the first time surpassing the output of the normally aspirated engines. By the time the turbo engines reached the apogee of their performance in the Lotus 98T of 1986, they were delivering twice that figure!

The 1979 season brought new cars for the Renault Sport team, which expanded to running two RS10 ground-effect cars for Jabouille and René Arnoux. Fittingly, Jabouille scored the car's – and turbocharging's – first victory at the French Grand Prix.

By this time turbocharging was firmly on the map. As rivals including BMW, Ferrari, Ford and Honda all moved to similar technology, Renault continued to clock up wins during the early 1980s. By the time Renault Sport withdrew from Formula 1 as a constructor in its own right at the end of the 1985 season, Jabouille, Arnoux and Alain Prost had chalked up no fewer than 15 victories, to which could be added the five wins scored in 1985 and 1986 by the Renault-powered Team Lotus cars of Elio de Angelis and Ayrton Senna.

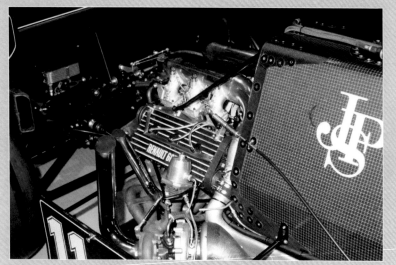

LEFT The first Lotus-Renault engine installation – the EF1 in the Lotus 93T.

(John Townsend, F1 Pictures)

COLIN CHAPMAN'S INFLUENCE

While not directly involved in the development of the turbocharged Lotus-Renault cars of the 1980s, Colin Chapman, before his fatal heart attack on 16 December 1982, had most certainly paved the way for the introduction of Renault power. It was Chapman, working with future team principal Peter Warr, who initiated discussions with the French car maker in the summer of 1982, and in its early stages the Lotus 93T certainly took shape under Chapman's eagle eye.

However, just as important as any physical legacy was the philosophy that Chapman created and fostered at Team Lotus. That philosophy – innovation, technical leadership, determination to win – continued long after Chapman's passing. It was once said that these principles were 'seared into the soul of every Team Lotus employee', creating a pride and competitive spirit that served the team well throughout the JPS Lotus-Renault turbo era.

BELOW Colin Chapman during the 1978 season – the year of Team Lotus's last World Championship title. *(John Townsend, F1 Pictures)*

The JPS turbo era begins

ABOVE A pensive Hazel Chapman, Elio de Angelis and Nigel Mansell at the launch of the Lotus 93T. *(John Townsend, F1 Pictures)*

Chapman began negotiations with Renault at a time when the factory's own Renault Sport team was at the peak of its form. During a 1982 season that produced 11 different winning drivers in seven different types of car, de Angelis in the Cosworth-powered JPS Lotus 91 won just a single race, while Renault team drivers Alain Prost and René Arnoux won four between them.

With a difficult financial climate in which car sales were reduced across Europe, Renault was reviewing its Formula 1 expenditure at this time and the prospect of becoming the engine supplier to a team with Team Lotus's credentials was attractive, while Team Lotus also needed to make a decisive move to keep its sponsor happy. The first JPS Lotus-Renault, the 93T, was designed by Martin Ogilvie with input from Chapman, making it the last car with which the Lotus boss was involved.

BELOW In the shelter of the team transporter, the Lotus 93T awaits its first track test at the Paul Ricard circuit in France. *(John Townsend, F1 Pictures)*

RIGHT For the first half of the 1983 season, Nigel Mansell drove the Cosworth DFY-powered Lotus 92, which featured computer-controlled active suspension. *(John Townsend, F1 Pictures)*

ABOVE Despite relaxed appearances, behind the scenes all was not well with the Lotus 93T. *(Classic Team Lotus)*

A new age

Following Chapman's death, control of Team Lotus passed to Competition Manager Peter Warr, who had been Chapman's right-hand man in Formula 1 since 1969. Warr was initially optimistic about the 1983 season when the 93T, on its first test runs at the Paul Ricard circuit in France, lapped 0.4sec faster than the best times of the Renault team cars. Just two examples of the 93T were built, to be driven by Elio de Angelis, who focused on the new turbo car's development during the first half of the season.

The team's second driver, Nigel Mansell, drove a Lotus 92, a stopgap car developed as an evolution of the previous year's Cosworth-powered design, utilising a Ford Cosworth DFY, a shorter-stroke version of the DFV. Even with the final Cosworth-powered cars, Team Lotus's spirit of inventiveness continued: in testing at the end of 1981 the team broke new ground by introducing 'active' suspension, whereby ride height was controlled by computers and hydro-pneumatic valves. Mansell raced with active suspension, the late Colin Chapman's final F1 design innovation, through the 1983 season.

Meanwhile, the turbocharged 93T performed relatively strongly in qualifying, but suffered seven retirements in the first eight races of the 1983 season, its only finish being de Angelis's ninth place in Belgium. In hindsight it appears that the Lotus engineers had underestimated the additional loads imposed on the

LEFT Elio de Angelis was tasked with developing the recalcitrant 93T. *(Classic Team Lotus)*

monocoque and gearbox by the more powerful engine, and in addition the late imposition of new flat-floor regulations to reduce downforce – when the design of the car was almost completed – meant that the Lotus 93T proved very much a compromise.

With John Player due to review its sponsorship agreement in the summer of 1983 amid a lack of early-season results for the team, Peter Warr was forced to move swiftly. He hired former Matra, Ligier and Alfa Romeo engineer Gérard Ducarouge, who proposed that the 93T be replaced by a 'new' design. With just six weeks to the British Grand Prix, which was set to be pivotal to the future of the John Player Specials, Ducarouge designed a new car, built around the composite Lotus 91 monocoque design of 1982, adapted to accommodate the Renault EF1 turbo engine.

The arrival of two Lotus 94Ts at Silverstone surprised many observers. The cars certainly looked different. They were longer, lower and leaner than the relatively short-wheelbase and frumpy 93T, and in addition to accommodating the Renault turbo V6 Ducarouge had incorporated some added details, such as reducing the size of the fuel cell as the car would now make refuelling pit-stops, benefiting overall weight and its distribution. Meanwhile, the John Player media machine lauded the 'unparalleled performance of British engineers to have built two brand-new cars in just six weeks', and only a few eagle-eyed onlookers noted the less sophisticated rocker-type front suspension that revealed the car's older design origins.

The new Lotus 94T acquitted itself well at Silverstone. De Angelis qualified on the second row of the grid only to suffer a turbo failure on just the second lap, but Mansell battled his way through from a lowly 18th on the grid to finish fourth, as Alain Prost's Renault took the chequered flag. Equally importantly for Team Lotus, the result convinced its sponsor that the team was on the right track and at the next grand prix, in Germany, a new contract was announced.

'We were a small group working to achieve the unachievable,' says Team Lotus mechanic Chris Dinnage, who was one of the team building the cars. 'The 94T got us out of trouble. The 93T just wasn't aerodynamically efficient. The 94T's smaller chassis meant we hadn't

ABOVE The Lotus 93T had distinctive angular bodywork following the lines of the monocoque beneath. *(Classic Team Lotus)*

BELOW Blistered rear tyres bear testimony to the handling issues with the 93T. *(John Townsend, F1 Pictures)*

but it succumbed to an oil pump failure after just 12 laps. Mansell qualified third and, despite being passed by Piquet and Prost, doggedly held that position for the final step on the podium.

It was clear that BMW, which had focused much of its attention on the development of special fuels containing chemicals such as toluene for its road-car-derived four-cylinder turbo engine, was giving Brabham a horsepower advantage. Other potential race-winning engines were also arriving on the scene: late in 1983 McLaren débuted its MP4/1E powered by a new bespoke 'TAG turbo' engine developed in association with Porsche while Williams was switching from Cosworth to turbocharged Honda horsepower for 1984.

Refinement and consistency – 1984

For the new season Ducarouge now had the comparative luxury of being able to develop a wholly new car. The resultant Lotus 95T was described by the Frenchman as 'a classical car', longer, slimmer and lighter than its predecessor. The longer wheelbase accommodated a larger 220-litre fuel tank as the rule-makers had now banned pit-stops, but the Nomex-cored, carbon-composite monocoque was lower and now featured the contemporary pull-rod front suspension. The rear of the car used a combined rocker arm and pull-rod suspension, specifically

ABOVE Just six weeks after the start of work on its design, the Lotus 94T was ready for its race début at Silverstone, where Elio de Angelis put it on the second row of the grid. *(Classic Team Lotus)*

enough fuel to finish a race, but with refuelling stops that wasn't an issue. The car had much more traction from the rear suspension.'

Team Lotus was now firmly in the midst of a five-way power struggle between the respective turbocharged teams. As Ferrari clinched the Constructors' title, the 1983 Drivers Championship went down to a last-race head-to-head in South Africa between Prost for Renault and Brabham-BMW driver Nelson Piquet. The Brazilian claimed the title by just two points after Prost retired.

The Lotus 94T's best race of the year came in the penultimate round of the season, the John Player-backed European Grand Prix at Brands Hatch. De Angelis put his car on pole position

RIGHT While the Lotus 95T still had an angular monocoque, smoother bodywork enhanced both appearance and airflow. *(John Townsend, F1 Pictures)*

designed to allow continued use of the existing
suspension pick-up points on the transaxle
casing, carried over from the previous model.

The 1984 season goes down in history as
one of McLaren domination. The TAG Turbo-
powered MP4/2 won 12 of the 16 races
as Niki Lauda beat his McLaren team-mate
Alain Prost, who had switched from Renault,
to the title by just half a championship point
(gained in the rain-drenched Monaco Grand
Prix which scored only half points after being
stopped prematurely). The Lotus 95T, however,
demonstrated its pace from the outset, with de
Angelis claiming pole position in the opening
round of the season in Brazil before eventually
finishing third in the race.

That opening race marked the start of a
frustrating pattern for Team Lotus. The 95T
proved the most consistent challenger to
McLaren through the season and de Angelis
was on the podium four times, including second
place in Detroit, on his way to third place in the
World Championship. However, he and Lotus
were not destined to taste victory. Mansell was
also quick: he enjoyed podium finishes with
third in France and Holland, and he also claimed
pole position in Dallas, only to have to attempt
to push the car across the line to salvage sixth
place after suffering gearbox problems.

While the Lotus 95T had good downforce and
handling, and its Renault EF4 engine was a match
for the rival TAG Turbo in terms of horsepower, its
higher fuel consumption meant that the Lotus cars
were heavier than the McLarens in the early stages
of a race. In addition, while Lotus had moved from
Pirelli to Goodyear tyres, they were still not a match
in grip and longevity to the similar Goodyears used
by McLaren.

CENTRE The Lotus 95T was longer than its
predecessor, to accommodate the 220-litre fuel
cell. *(John Townsend, F1 Pictures)*

RIGHT The 95T put Team Lotus on a par with
Williams in 1984, but it could do little against the
all-conquering McLarens. *(Classic Team Lotus)*

Ultimately, the Lotus's weakness was reliability. Even after upgrades to the gearbox to enhance rigidity, improve lubrication and strengthen its selectors, this was to prove a crucial weak point, and one that was probably not helped by Mansell's aggressive driving style. Mansell was capable on his day of outpacing his Italian team-mate but was described by correspondent Alan Henry as 'yet to refine his over-ambitious driving style' and perhaps a

record of just five finishes (albeit all in the points) from 16 races tells its own story.

The relationship between Mansell and team boss Peter Warr was at best stony and the 1984 Monaco Grand Prix marked a low point. Held on a track soaked by torrential rain, this race saw Mansell pass pole-sitter Alain Prost and lead for six laps, only to lose control and clash with the barrier on the climb to Casino Square. Frustrated at the loss of victory, Warr was famously quoted as commenting, 'He'll never win a grand prix as long as I have a hole in my arse.' Of course, Mansell's eventual tally of 31 victories would prove Warr's comment to be completely wrong.

The bigger story of the Monaco race was the performance of Brazilian rookie Ayrton Senna in the unfancied Toleman-Hart. In just his sixth grand prix, Senna was closing fast on Prost when the chequered flag was shown early, stopping the race on the 31st of the planned 76 laps with Prost the lucky winner.

Just a few weeks later there was a confidential meeting in London attended by Peter Warr, Peter Dyke (John Player's head of sponsorship) and Senna. A deal was struck and the young Brazilian was hired to drive alongside de Angelis for the 1985 season. As a consequence Mansell left the team that 'gave him his break' in Formula 1 and joined Keke Rosberg at Williams-Honda.

The 1985 season began a new chapter with Senna and Team Lotus. The Lotus 97T and 98T were destined to become the ultimate JPS Lotus-Renault grand prix cars.

PETER WARR

Regarded by many as the backbone of Team Lotus, Peter Warr provided cool and incisive management even when Colin Chapman was still nominally in control, and Warr's combination of acumen and discipline propelled the team forward after he took over the role of team principal following Chapman's death. It was Warr who guided the relationship with Renault and managed the demands of John Player, while at the same time pushing the limits both in terms of technology and on the track. Tall, bespectacled and with a ramrod-straight bearing that led many to think he had been a Guards officer, Warr demanded, and achieved, respect up and down the Formula 1 pitlane.

Warr had indeed been a graduate of the Royal Military College at Sandhurst, but his intended career with the Royal Horse Artillery (where his mathematical skills would have served him well as a gunnery officer) was curtailed by a leg injury. Upon being 'demobbed' in 1958, he – in his own words – 'scrounged' a job as assistant sales manager for Lotus sports cars in Hornsey.

Warr was himself no mean racer. He campaigned a Lotus Seven that had been specially built for Graham Hill to drive at the traditional Boxing Day Brands Hatch fixture in 1959. He then switched to the single-seater Formula Junior category in which he won the 1962 *Eiffelrennen* at the Nürburgring at the wheel of a Lotus 20. A distinctive achievement came at the inaugural Japanese Grand Prix, held in 1963 at Suzuka as a sports car event that Warr won in a Lotus 23B.

Warr parted company with Lotus in 1966, principally because the job to which he aspired, Lotus F1 manager, had been given by Chapman to his colleague Andrew Ferguson. After three years running a Scalextric slot car racing centre, Warr was tipped off by Ferguson that he was leaving the team. Warr rejoined in late 1969 and managed the team through the golden years of the Lotus 72, playing a key role in Jochen Rindt's posthumous title of 1970 and Emerson Fittipaldi's successful 1972 campaign that marked a rebirth of the team, with Fittipaldi becoming the then youngest-ever World Champion.

Warr left Team Lotus again in 1976, attracted by the opportunity to build a 'clean-sheet' racing team for Canadian oil millionaire Walter Wolf and South African driver Jody Scheckter. The Wolf Racing Team rocked the establishment when Scheckter won the first race of the 1977 season and continued to perform well enough to claim second place in that year's World Championship.

By 1981 Warr was back at Team Lotus after what Chapman joked was 'just a brief sabbatical'. Following Chapman's death, Warr took the helm and stamped his authority upon the team. Some complained that he could be sharp and overbearing, others that his background in focusing on the logistical side of the team meant that he could not delegate well and tended to micro-manage. What was clear, though, is that he turned Team Lotus back into winners.

It was Warr who persuaded Renault to develop its relationship with Team Lotus from being just a 'customer' team to becoming the official factory operation. It was Warr who spotted the availability of Gérard Ducarouge and hired him to transform the design of the team's cars. And it was Warr who secured Ayrton Senna's services despite John Player being pro-Mansell. Just two races into 1985, Senna scored the first win of Team Lotus's post-Chapman era and, perhaps fittingly, he also claimed the team's last grand prix victory, in Detroit in 1987.

Warr left Team Lotus for the last time in 1989. He became secretary of the British Racing Drivers' Club at Silverstone and permanent F1 steward for the FIA, before retiring to France where he died, aged 72, on 4 October 2010.

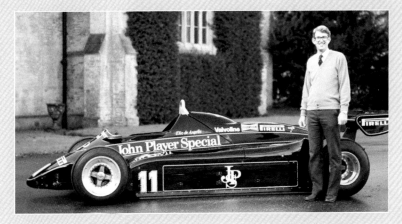

BELOW Peter Warr at Ketteringham Hall, Team Lotus's HQ, with the Lotus 91. *(John Townsend, F1 Pictures)*

Chapter Two

The Senna years

The 1985 and 1986 World Championship seasons are reckoned by many to have been among the most open and closely fought in the history of Formula 1. Team Lotus was well placed to reap the benefits, having moved quickly to sign Ayrton Senna, Formula 1's sensational new star. Lotus's Renault-powered cars were the 97T (1985) and 98T (1986), the latter the fastest-ever Lotus and one of the most powerful grand prix cars ever built.

OPPOSITE Senna in all his glory, hustling his Lotus 98T to third place in the 1986 Monaco Grand Prix.
(John Townsend, F1 Pictures)

Regarded by many as the definitive racing driver, triple World Champion Ayrton Senna honed his Formula 1 race-winning skills at the helm of the JPS Lotus 97T and 98T cars, although his destiny was already set when he signed his contract with Team Lotus in the late summer of 1984.

Senna was born on 21 March 1960 into a family at the heart of São Paulo's fast-growing technocracy. The middle child of factory owner Milton da Silva and his wife Neide Senna da Silva, Ayrton, along with elder sister Viviane and younger brother Leonardo, was brought up in a house owned by Neide's father, João Senna, who owned the adjacent aeronautical materials and engineering park and airport that fostered Ayrton's interest in aircraft, cars and technology from the outset.

RIGHT Ayrton Senna – his first four grand prix wins came with Team Lotus. *(John Townsend, F1 Pictures)*

BELOW Senna and race engineer Steve Hallam. *(John Townsend, F1 Pictures)*

Senna was introduced to the world of motorsport by karting. He entered his first competition at Interlagos just after his 13th birthday. He qualified for his first-ever race on pole position and held the lead before retiring after a collision with a rival. A few weeks later, however, Senna took the chequered flag at Interlagos on 1 July 1973 for his first victory.

Clearly the support of a wealthy family was an advantage, but raw talent also shone through. Senna won the South American Kart Championship in 1977, before moving to Europe where he contested the Karting World Championship between 1978 and 1982. He raced principally for the Parilla brothers, Angelo and Achille, whose DAP team was at the top of the karting tree.

To Senna's frustration, he finished runner-up in the 1979 and 1980 Karting World Championships, but by 1981 he had gone into car racing. He moved to Norfolk to begin a season of Formula Ford 1600 with Van Diemen and lived just a few miles from his future employer at Team Lotus. Such was Ayrton's pace that in his début year he won 12 of 19 races and finished the season as a double champion, winning both the RAC British and BRSCC Townsend Thoresen titles. After a brief sabbatical in Brazil managing his father's building company, he returned for 1982 to win both the British and European Formula Ford 2000 championships with a tally of 22 wins from 27 races, plus 23 fastest laps and 16 poles.

By now he was using a new name. Ayrton had previously raced as 'Senna da Silva' but realised it was too long for commentators to publicise him and to fit on his pit board. He felt that 'da Silva' was too common a name in Brazil, so instead he adopted his mother's maiden name of Senna.

For the 1983 season he moved up to the Marlboro British Formula 3 Championship, regarded as the ultimate stepping stone to Formula 1. Driving for Dick Bennetts in a West Surrey Racing Ralt-Toyota, Senna competed in 21 races, finishing the year with 13 wins, 15 pole positions and, after a season-long battle with the Eddie Jordan-entered Ralt of Martin Brundle, the title. Adding to his accolades, Senna went on to win the prestigious end-of-season Macau Grand Prix.

Formula 1 beckoned and during the 1983 season Senna was given test drives with Williams, McLaren, Brabham and Toleman. As a result, Peter Warr of Team Lotus, Ron Dennis of McLaren and Bernie Ecclestone of Brabham all offered Senna a test-driving role for 1984, with an opportunity to race in 1985, but Ayrton turned them down in favour of Toleman, who would let him race right away.

Senna's début, as team-mate to former world motorcycle racing champion Johnny Cecotto, was hardly auspicious. He qualified 17th for the Brazilian Grand Prix and became the first retirement of the 1984 season with a turbo failure on the eighth lap. His first World Championship point came in his second race, with sixth place in the South African Grand Prix, and he scored again in Belgium.

The race that brought Senna to the world's attention was the rain-soaked Monaco Grand Prix. After qualifying 13th, he overtook rivals with seeming impunity and reached second place. He was closing on race leader Alain Prost at a rate of four seconds a lap until the race was stopped prematurely because of the torrential rain.

While Senna's charge is now history, it was his pace and precision in other races that gained him the respect of his peers. Pat Symonds, his race engineer at Toleman, remembers the Detroit Grand Prix, where Senna retired after clipping a wall.

'Senna said, "I'm sure the wall moved." Even though I've heard every driver excuse, I certainly hadn't heard that one! But he was absolutely right: someone had hit the far end of a concrete block and that made it swivel slightly, so the leading edge of the block was standing out by a few millimetres. Senna was driving with such precision that those few millimetres were the difference between hitting the wall and not hitting it.'

Ayrton went on to claim two podium positions, with third place in the British and Portuguese Grands Prix, but was suspended from the Italian Grand Prix by a furious Toleman management when they discovered that he had been in talks with John Player and Team Lotus about the forthcoming season.

At Team Lotus's photo-call at a chilly Donington Park, Senna stared stony-faced at the camera. Team Lotus mechanic Chris Dinnage recalls the reason: 'He arrived at that first photo-shoot suffering from Bell's palsy, which left him with a frozen face. He and Elio de Angelis got on really well, although as the season went by Elio became frustrated he couldn't match Ayrton's pace. Elio had started with the mantle of top dog, but Ayrton stole his thunder.'

After his three seasons with Team Lotus, Senna moved to McLaren-Honda and began a winning streak that saw him claim three World Championship titles and 35 victories with the team. He moved to Williams-Renault for his final, ill-fated season and tragically lost his life on 1 May 1994 in the San Marino Grand Prix at Imola.

Ayrton Senna was a man of contrasts. Much is made of his ferocious rivalry with McLaren team-mate Alain Prost and, equally, of Senna's multi-million dollar legacy funding support to the poor in Brazil. He also could be frustratingly off-hand with those around him if they were not directly involved in advancing his success. Yet, at a more fundamental level, he won the respect of those who worked with him.

'He was very motivated,' says Chris Dinnage. 'Ayrton would stay in the pit garage with us until 10 or 11 at night, until everything was right.'

There was another side to Senna's relationship with his mechanics. After one pre-season test in Brazil, Senna picked them up from Rio in a minibus and drove them to his holiday home at Ubatuba, near São Paulo.

'It was throwing it down with rain,' Dinnage remembers. 'Ayrton was driving, we were in the back. When he stopped to refuel, it was him out in the rain, filling the tank. You don't get many World Champions doing that.'

BELOW Ayrton Senna poses with his engine builders at Viry-Châtillon in 1986. *(Renault Sport)*

The 1985 season

The 1985 season opened with Ayrton Senna making his JPS Lotus-Renault début alongside established team driver Elio de Angelis. Reigning champions McLaren were favourites to continue the run of success that had put Niki Lauda and Alain Prost at the top of the previous year's standings. The new Williams-Honda pairing of Keke Rosberg and Nigel Mansell looked likely to provide strong opposition. At Ferrari, while there were cracks forming in the relationship with René Arnoux, Michele Alboreto was set to become a season-long front-runner.

The new JPS car for the 1985 season skipped one number in the Lotus type-numbering sequence. The Lotus 96 was a stillborn Cosworth-powered CART Indycar project designed by Gérard Ducarouge, but due to contractual setbacks the sole prototype was never raced. So it was that the new Formula 1 car became the Lotus 97T.

The 97T was able to utilise both the previous season's Renault EF4 turbocharged engine and an updated version, the EF15, which featured more power and better throttle response in qualifying. By utilising a smaller bore and longer stroke, the new engine was also able to deliver improved fuel consumption at lower boost levels.

Fuel management proved to be a critical factor during the 1985 season. As in 1984, no in-race refuelling was allowed and race performance was therefore constrained by the maximum fuel-tank size of 220 litres, with the drivers controlling fuel consumption by raising or lowering turbo boost pressure via a control

CENTRE Ayrton Senna, face frozen after an attack of Bell's palsy, and Elio de Angelis pose with the Lotus 97T ahead of a shakedown at Donington Park. *(Classic Team Lotus)*

LEFT Third and fourth on the grid for the opening race of 1985, the Brazilian Grand Prix. *(Classic Team Lotus)*

on the steering wheel. For qualifying, though, there were no such restrictions and horsepower figures on full boost soared past 1,000bhp.

The opening race of the 1985 season in Rio de Janeiro, Brazil, demonstrated that both Team Lotus drivers had the pace to challenge for victory. Alboreto claimed pole position for Ferrari closely followed by Rosberg's Williams, then Senna and de Angelis lined up third and fourth on the grid. In the race Senna retired with electrical problems but de Angelis finished a promising third behind Prost's McLaren and Alboreto's Ferrari.

Senna makes his mark

It was just the second round of the World Championship when Senna stamped his authority on both his new team and the world of Formula 1. The Portuguese Grand Prix, held at Estoril near Lisbon on 21 April 1985, was marked by torrential rain, but Senna first made his mark with a stunning qualifying lap that put him on pole position more than 0.4sec faster than Prost's second-placed McLaren and over a second faster than his team-mate de Angelis. Senna then simply crushed the opposition in the race, with a dominant performance that saw him lap every car in the field except the second-

RIGHT For the wet conditions in Portugal, the team raised the ride height to prevent the floor from causing aquaplaning. *(John Townsend, F1 Pictures)*

ABOVE **Delight for Senna at Estoril, Portugal, as he scores his first grand prix win.** *(John Townsend, F1 Pictures)*

BELOW **Peter Warr's joy is clear as Senna drives into the Portuguese paddock.** *(Classic Team Lotus)*

BELOW RIGHT **Senna's first time on the Formula 1 winner's podium was a moment to savour.** *(John Townsend, F1 Pictures)*

placed Ferrari of Alboreto, which was still more than a minute behind.

Among the lapped drivers was de Angelis, who started, and finished, fourth. As Alan Henry, F1 correspondent for *The Guardian* newspaper, subsequently wrote: 'De Angelis's frustration was almost tangible as he chased Senna as hard as he could in the other 97T, but there was simply no way he could compete. The penny must have dropped in Elio's mind that, his status usurped by this newcomer, he no longer had a future with the team that had been his home since the start of 1980.'

De Angelis's final flourish

In terms of the final results, the third round of the season, the San Marino Grand Prix at Imola in northern Italy, could perhaps be judged to have levelled the balance, with de Angelis being classified as the winner. In fact, the real race was again between Senna and Prost.

JPS Team Lotus, working with Renault, had adopted a strategy of using the earlier short-stroke EF4 engine working with unlimited boost to give maximum power in qualifying, before switching to the newly revised Renault EF15 unit for the race, as the EF15 offered lower fuel consumption. Senna duly utilised the EF4 to claim pole position, ahead of Rosberg's Williams and de Angelis in the second Lotus 97T.

Senna led from the start, while de Angelis hustled his sister JPS car into second place. The Italian knew, even with the benefit of the EF15 engine, that if he tried to maintain Senna's early pace he would end up dangerously short of fuel, so he dropped back, eventually being caught and passed by Prost, who was charging through the field from sixth place. By lap 24 Prost was on Senna's tail, lunging and diving in his attempts to pass, each move parried by Senna. Eventually Prost, too, became concerned about fuel consumption and reduced his pace, while Senna also slowed for the same reason.

There were further twists to come. Due to lack of supply of EF15 race engines, Senna's

car was still fitted with the earlier, thirstier EF4 engine, and despite the Brazilian's best economy-driving efforts, including coasting into the corners, the Lotus's fuel tanks ran dry with three laps to go. Prost inherited the victory, but he ran out of fuel on the slowing-down lap and post-race scrutineering revealed that the bone-dry McLaren was 2kg under the minimum weight allowed, and was duly excluded. That returned victory to Team Lotus and de Angelis, the only other driver to have completed all 60 racing laps. It was de Angelis's second grand prix win, and, as it would turn out, his last.

Senna was back in the thick of the action at the Monaco Grand Prix, where he again claimed pole position by just 0.086sec from his Team Lotus predecessor Nigel Mansell. Once again, though, the Brazilian was denied a finish when his engine, which had been 'buzzed' to the rev limiter when it jumped out of gear in the pre-race morning warm-up session, expired on the 13th lap. As Prost and Alboreto battled for first and second places, an unsung hero of the race was de Angelis, who fought his way from ninth at the start to claim third place for Team Lotus at the chequered flag.

Practice pace, reliability woes

The postponement of the Belgian Grand Prix until later in the season, due to the new Spa circuit's inadequate track surface, meant that the next race on the calendar became the

Canadian Grand Prix, and for the first time in the season Senna did not head the qualifying times. It was de Angelis instead who claimed pole position, 0.289sec ahead of the Brazilian; it was the last-ever qualifying 1–2 for Team Lotus.

There was to be no fairytale ending in Canada. Senna was eventually classified five laps down after suffering a turbo problem and, despite leading the race, de Angelis was eventually forced to settle for fourth. As the season developed, so did a familiar pattern for the JPS Lotus team, with Senna either on pole position or near the top in qualifying, but with reliability problems frustrating both drivers during the races. Although de Angelis could not match Senna's aggressive pace, his lighter touch often allowed him to secure a top-six finish as Senna retired.

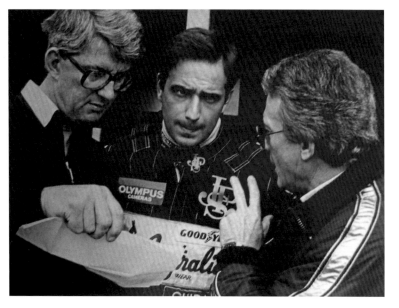

LEFT Elio de Angelis's frustration became increasingly evident as the 1985 season progressed. Here he is seen with Peter Warr (left) and Gérard Ducarouge. *(Classic Team Lotus)*

On the Detroit street circuit Senna again claimed pole, but was set to end his race in the retaining wall after a rare error, while de Angelis finished fifth.

Then at the Paul Ricard track in France, Senna qualified second and in the race he initially pursued pole-sitter Rosberg, only to feel his engine lose its edge. He dived into the pits for attention and after rejoining, racing hard to make up ground, the engine exploded at the entrance to the fast Signes corner at the end of

ELIO DE ANGELIS

A proud Roman with an aristocratic background and a cultured upbringing, Elio de Angelis was an integral part of Team Lotus from 1980 to 1985 and, with 94 starts, he drove more races for the team than any other driver. He took the team from normally aspirated Cosworth DFV power through the transition to the turbo cars and he scored both of his grand prix victories at the wheel of JPS-Lotus cars.

Born on 26 March 1958, de Angelis inherited his competitive instincts from his father Giulio, a successful powerboat racer, crewing for

RIGHT Elio de Angelis – long-standing, loyal Team Lotus driver who became overshadowed by Senna in 1985. *(John Townsend, F1 Pictures)*

him before switching first to karts and then to Formula 3, where he claimed the Italian Championship in 1977. In 1978 he raced in Formula 2 for Minardi and also won the prestigious Monaco Formula 3 race, before moving to Formula 1 in 1979 with the Shadow team, scoring a best result of fourth place in the final race of the season, the United States Grand Prix at Watkins Glen.

For the 1980 season he moved to Team Lotus as number two to 1978 World Champion Mario Andretti. At least that was the theory. In fact de Angelis out-qualified his illustrious team-mate in eight of the 14 races and scored 13 points for sixth place in the championship, whereas Andretti, increasingly disillusioned after a string of engine and gearbox woes, scored just one point. A highlight for de Angelis that year was his first podium finish, for second place to René Arnoux in the Brazilian Grand Prix; had he been able to make up the 21-second margin to the victorious Renault driver he would have become, at 21 years and 10 months, the youngest grand prix winner of the time.

It took until the 1982 season for de Angelis to score his first victory, a memorable success at the 1982 Austrian Grand Prix when he finished less than half a car length and only 0.05sec ahead of Keke Rosberg's McLaren. It was also the last win to be hailed by Colin

the mile-long Mistral straight. It dumped oil on to the rear tyres, causing the car to spin out of the race and crash at over 200mph. De Angelis slipped home fourth.

Bruised but unbowed, Senna was back in contention at the British Grand Prix even if his qualifying thunder was stolen by Rosberg's record pole-position lap at an average speed of 160.9mph, a Formula 1 record that was to stand unbroken for 17 years. Senna qualified only fourth, but in the race he rapidly moved into the lead and held it until the 60th of 65 laps when he coasted to a standstill. In response Chapman's famous act of throwing his cap into the air at the finish. With the passing of Chapman and the arrival of turbo power at the end of 1982, Team Lotus entered a new era.

The 1983 season brought no fewer than 12 mechanically related non-finishes, but by the following year de Angelis and Team Lotus were again among the front-runners. No victories were scored by the Italian, his best result being second place on the Detroit street circuit, but he comfortably outpaced team-mate Nigel Mansell on his way to third place in the Drivers' Championship behind Niki Lauda and Alain Prost.

Ayrton Senna joined de Angelis at Team Lotus for 1985. Initially the two drivers appeared closely matched and certainly worked well together. However, there was inevitable frustration as Senna's pace and confidence soared and de Angelis struggled to match him. Elio's victory at the San Marino Grand Prix in May 1985 would be his last. A year later, after moving to Brabham-BMW for the new season, he was killed on 15 May 1986 in a testing accident at the Paul Ricard circuit.

'Elio was perceived as a bit of a rich boy, but he was really good,' remembers Chris Dinnage. 'Once Mario left, Elio was top dog. But when Ayrton arrived, he stole Elio's thunder. The longer the season went on, the more Elio got frustrated that he couldn't match Senna's pace.

It was a pity. Against everyone else, he'd proved he was a top-class driver.'

Journalist and Team Lotus PR and sponsorship agent Andrew Marriott also has good memories of Elio de Angelis: 'He was a fantastic guy – urbane, cultured and intelligent. Lots of people comment that he was also a classical pianist, but it was just one of many talents. He was very much an upper-class Italian and some have called him "the last of the gentlemen racers", which he was. But he was also a very quick and committed racer.'

BELOW **Elio de Angelis's white Simpson helmet was distinctive for its 'Darth Vader' style.** *(John Townsend, F1 Pictures)*

to a faulty electronic sensor, the engine had adjusted the fuel/air mixture control to fully rich and the increased fuel consumption had run the tank dry.

Changeable weather conditions at the Nürburgring gave the Toleman of Teo Fabi a surprise pole position with Senna qualifying fifth and de Angelis seventh. Ultimately victory went to Alboreto's Ferrari as both Lotuses retired, Senna with a failed driveshaft coupling and de Angelis with engine failure.

The rain-soaked Austrian Grand Prix saw Prost's McLaren claim pole as Senna struggled in a lowly 14th place after mechanical problems. The real dramas, however, began with a start-line pile-up that caused the race to be red-flagged, a number of drivers, including de Angelis, then scrambling to replace their wrecked machines with spare cars. The restarted race saw de Angelis in the spare car come home a creditable fifth, but he was again overshadowed by Senna, who charged though the field to finish second to the seemingly imperturbable Prost. It was another sign of Senna's emerging talent and racing aggression.

The twisting Zandvoort circuit in Holland saw the Brabham-BMW of Nelson Piquet claim pole position only to lose his advantage by stalling on the start line. At the finish Senna claimed third place behind a McLaren 1–2 for Lauda and Prost, while de Angelis was fifth.

Senna back on top

The Italian Grand Prix at Monza saw Senna back on top in qualifying, claiming his fifth pole position of the season at an average speed of 152.487mph. The Lotus was unable to maintain

its advantage in the race, however, with Senna finishing third and de Angelis sixth as Prost took victory, moving ahead of Alboreto in the Drivers' Championship.

The Belgian Grand Prix at the fast, swooping and demanding Spa-Francorchamps circuit saw Senna turn the tables. While Prost claimed pole from Senna by just 0.097sec, in a classic Spa race with the track alternating between wet and dry conditions, Senna was in a class of his own, claiming his second grand prix victory by 28sec from the Williams of Nigel Mansell. De Angelis, who qualified ninth, retired with turbo failure.

The European Grand Prix saw Senna claim another spectacular pole position in the 97T, making the first-ever lap of Brands Hatch at an average of over 140mph. The Brazilian started strongly, but canny strategy from the Williams team saw Rosberg, a lap down after a tyre stop, released from the pits just ahead of Senna. Rosberg slowed the Brazilian, allowing Mansell in the second-placed Williams to catch up. A few laps later Mansell dived into the lead at Paddock Hill bend and headed to a popular maiden victory in front of a euphoric home crowd.

Team Lotus race director Peter Warr was naturally furious and wanted to lodge a protest that Mansell had overtaken Senna while yellow warning flags were being waved. It could have led to the Briton's exclusion, but Hazel Chapman, Colin's widow, intervened in support of the former JPS driver. She quietly but firmly said, 'We are not going to protest Nigel', and thus the victory stood uncontested.

ABOVE Second on the grid at Spa, Senna outraced rival Prost to claim his second Grand Prix victory. *(Classic Team Lotus)*

LEFT Back home in Hethel, Senna's Spa win was front-page news – and the sponsor's message was ever-present. *(Classic Team Lotus)*

LEFT A dramatic European Grand Prix saw Senna pipped by Nigel Mansell. It was said Mansell had passed under yellow flags, but Hazel Chapman refused to countenance a protest. *(Classic Team Lotus)*

The next race in South Africa again saw Mansell and Williams on top, claiming both pole position and victory as Senna and de Angelis suffered engine failures.

The potential of the Team Lotus and Senna combination for the forthcoming new season was again demonstrated in the final race of 1985, at the newly commissioned Adelaide street circuit in Australia. Initially Rosberg and

Mansell's Williams cars headed the qualifying times, trading thousandths of a second for superiority, but then on a single flying lap at the very end of the final qualifying session Senna stunned everyone by lapping 0.704sec faster to claim an emphatic pole.

The race itself saw Rosberg score his final win for Williams before moving to McLaren for 1986. Senna had to drop out after another engine failure while de Angelis was given the black flag and disqualified because, after a delay on the warming-up lap, he regained his grid position instead of starting from the back. He later confessed that in the heat of the moment he 'simply forgot the rules'. It was a disappointing final Team Lotus outing for de Angelis, who moved to Brabham for 1986.

With Senna now indisputably 'number one' in the team and a car with proven pace, the prospects for JPS Team Lotus in 1986 looked rosy indeed.

The 1986 season

In the build-up to the 1986 season Ayrton Senna's dominance within Team Lotus had a serious influence on the team line-up for the coming year. Following the departure of de Angelis, it was assumed by many that Derek

Warwick, left jobless after Renault disbanded its race team, would be the natural replacement.

Warwick's appointment, however, was vetoed by Senna, who expressed doubts about whether Team Lotus, faced with a massive technical challenge from Williams-Honda as well as reigning champions TAG McLaren, would have the resources to field two reliable front-running cars for two top-line drivers. Better, said Senna, to have one front-runner and employ a more junior driver to help develop the new technologies.

Peter Warr had little choice but to accede and Johnny Dumfries became Senna's team-mate. Dumfries had won 14 races on his way to clinching the 1984 British Formula 3 Championship, Britain's top junior racing category, and in 1985 he had gained further experience in the inaugural International Formula 3000 Championship for cars using a detuned version of the now-obsolete Cosworth DFV Formula 1 engine. However, Dumfries now had to handle a step-up in horsepower from around 400bhp to more than double that amount with the new turbo cars.

The new Lotus 98T was in some respects an evolution of the previous year's car, which, despite the fuel consumption shortcomings of its Renault engine, was generally regarded as being among the most aerodynamically efficient and best-handling chassis on the grid. The monocoque

of the 98T, however, was subtly different in construction from that of its predecessor.

While still utilising carbonfibre and Kevlar sandwich, bonded around aluminium bulkheads, the new car had a one-piece moulded 'tub'. The new construction increased rigidity and reduced weight, although the car still used a separate non-structural outer body cover.

Unlimited boost

Additional, removable lower engine-cover panels on the 98T replaced the earlier higher-sided rear monocoque, to allow easier access to turbochargers and the wastegates that controlled engine boost pressure. This was an important development as the access allowed the cars to run during qualifying with wastegates removed and blanked off, giving unlimited boost levels, which resulted in power outputs in excess of 1,100bhp at over 5.0 bar of pressure.

For the new season, only the Renault EF15 engine would be used, upgraded to 'bis' specification and, later in the season, able to reach higher revs after the introduction of pneumatically controlled valvegear.

There were also visual differences between the 97T and the 98T. Behind the driver's head the engine cover was raised slightly on the 98T, both to smooth airflow to the rear aerofoils and to accommodate a larger

ABOVE Johnny Dumfries's prime role during the 1986 season was to develop the new six-speed gearbox. *(John Townsend, F1 Pictures)*

Economy drive

While qualifying was unlimited in terms of turbo boost and horsepower, the 16 races making up the 1986 season would still be defined by fuel economy, with the rule-makers further constraining consumption by reducing the maximum fuel cell size from 220 to 195 litres. As in previous seasons, the drivers would attempt to control usage by steering-wheel-mounted turbo boost controls, aided by a cockpit read-out that gave more accurate information of fuel burn.

Winter testing confirmed that the four-cylinder BMW turbo unit used by Brabham had potentially the highest overall horsepower, but the Honda engine in the Williams car seemed to offer the ideal compromise between power and fuel efficiency, ahead of Renault and the TAG turbo unit used by reigning champions McLaren. Team Lotus, however, was confident that the Gérard Ducarouge-designed 98T was a leader in handling and aerodynamic efficiency.

The season-opening Brazilian Grand Prix at Jacarepaguá in Rio de Janeiro appeared to confirm predictions. Senna blasted to pole position by a very comfortable 0.76sec margin

ABOVE Senna was indisputably number-one driver for 1986. *(John Townsend, F1 Pictures)*

BELOW The 1986 championship turned into a fight between Lotus, Williams and McLaren. *(John Townsend, F1 Pictures)*

plenum chamber on the Renault EF15 engine. The distinctive trapezoidal front wings of the 97T were replaced with parallel-chord aerofoils. In response to a regulation change that outlawed 'bunny ear' supplementary winglets on the front of the rear-wing endplates (used at tracks where downforce mattered more than drag considerations), the 98T had a revised rear wing with the option of adding a smaller second element below the main aerofoil section.

from Nelson Piquet, Williams-Honda's new signing, but after leading the first three laps in the race Senna, driving to the indications given by his fuel monitor, was powerless to prevent his compatriot from passing and heading to victory. As Brazilian fans celebrated a 1–2 result for their countrymen, Renault, though outgunned on fuel economy, was at least pleased with the reliability of its engine. As well as the two Lotus cars that were the focus of Renault's factory efforts, all four of the 'customer' Renault engines powering the Ligier and Tyrrell entries took the chequered flag. Dumfries, meanwhile, completed his début grand prix in a creditable ninth place.

One key difference between the two Lotus 98Ts was the gearbox. For the new season Senna had opted to stick with the proven Lotus/Hewland DGB five-speed transmission on grounds of reliability, while Dumfries was tasked with development of a new six-speed gearbox. The next race, the inaugural Formula 1 event at Jerez in southern Spain, confirmed Senna's foresight, as Dumfries, after qualifying tenth, was forced out of the race by transmission failure, while Senna won one of the most closely fought races in grand prix history.

Spanish shoot-out

Senna again dominated qualifying at Jerez, claiming Team Lotus's 100th pole position from Piquet by a huge 0.83sec margin and then converting his starting position into an early-race lead. Senna then began to set his pace according to the fuel read-out on the car's dashboard display and it rapidly became clear that the Williams-Honda of Nigel Mansell was going to be a major threat.

Mansell had also been on an 'economy

ABOVE Despite the bravado of the flag marshal in Brazil, the new local hero was merely second, not the winner. *(John Townsend, F1 Pictures)*

LEFT Senna's first win of 1986 came in the second race of the season at Jerez in Spain. *(John Townsend, F1 Pictures)*

drive' in the early stages of the race, dropping from third to fifth, but a mid-race charge saw the Briton pass Senna on lap 39 and rapidly pull out a lead of 3.5 seconds. Then Mansell's luck changed as his car's handling began to deteriorate on the 68th of 72 laps. Suspecting a slow puncture, the Williams team called him in for a tyre change. Senna, still driving to his 'gas

JOHNNY DUMFRIES

Ayrton Senna's team-mate and the only other driver to race the definitive Lotus 98T was the Earl of Dumfries, who preferred to be called simply Johnny Dumfries.

John Colum Crichton-Stuart was born on 26 April 1958 into one of Scotland's oldest aristocratic families. He is a descendant of Robert II of Scotland (and through him Robert the Bruce) and of Kings Charles II and William IV of England, and he is also a distant cousin of Queen Elizabeth II. Today he carries the hereditary title of the 7th Marquess of Bute.

Behind the aristocratic titles, Dumfries was a worker. He had left the exclusive Ampleforth College early, working as a painter/decorator and a van driver while racing first in karts, then in Formula Ford. Dumfries made his Formula 3 début in 1983, the year in which Senna dominated the championship, the young Briton coming to the motorsport world's attention when he fought a spectacular battle with Senna for second place in a European Championship round at Silverstone.

'Martin Brundle walked that race,' Dumfries later told Motor Sport magazine. 'Ayrton made a very tricky tyre choice and it really didn't work. He put me on the bloody grass at full speed going down to Stowe, which wasn't a great experience.' Eventually Dumfries began to suffer a sticking throttle, but it didn't prevent him breaking the lap record, before he finally retired when the throttle problem caused him to over-rev the engine.

That drive helped secure Dumfries a place for 1984 in David Price's BP Formula 3 team. He was the sensation of the season, scoring 14 victories on his way to the title and, despite missing several races, he finished a close second to future Ferrari driver Ivan Capelli in the European Championship, beating the likes of Gerhard Berger, Roberto Ravaglia, Kris Nissen and John Nielsen.

Dumfries tested for Lotus, Brabham, Williams and McLaren as part of his prize for winning the Formula 3 title, but for 1985 he chose to take a testing role with Ferrari – he later described it as 'the romantic option' – and combined this with an abbreviated season in the International Formula 3000 Championship.

'In retrospect I was naive!' Dumfries recalls. 'I should have gone for a contract offered by Brabham, but I took the Ferrari deal. I didn't like mileage', regained the lead, closely followed by Prost in the McLaren. When Mansell rejoined he was third, more than 15 seconds behind the leading duo.

What followed was the stuff of legend. Mansell, lapping over three seconds a lap faster than the race leaders, caught and passed Prost on lap 70, and quickly closed on Senna's Lotus. The start of the last lap of the race saw Mansell just 1.5 seconds behind, but Senna, described as 'driving on his consumption gauge and his mirrors', positioned his car to block Mansell's last-corner charge.

Being forced to take the long way round proved decisive for Mansell. The two cars crossed the finish line side-by-side, with Mansell's car taking the lead just a metre beyond the line. Critically, the two cars' electronic timing transponders gave the verdict to Senna, by just 0.014sec!

'I realised he had stopped and he had new tyres,' said Senna. 'My tyres were gone. I had to really push with no grip, I was sideways, sideways, sideways, I nearly lost the car. I thought I had lost it, then it came back!'

The next race, the San Marino Grand

Fiorano very much. It's a really tiny little track, with a housing estate on one side – the location is quite weird and surreal. The car was difficult to drive as well. The object of the exercise for them was to develop their four-cylinder engine, but the project got shelved, and after a couple of months I didn't do any more testing.'

That decision could have ended Dumfries's Formula 1 career, but then came the chance to join Team Lotus as Senna's team-mate for the 1986 season. After Senna vetoed Peter Warr's first choice of Derek Warwick, who had tested for the team late in the 1985 season, Dumfries was in the perfect place to pick up the drive.

'There was nothing personal against Warwick,' recalls Team Lotus mechanic Chris Dinnage, 'but Ayrton didn't want to have an equal number one driver. He wanted all the team's efforts and resources focused on him. Johnny was a good bloke, in the right place at the right time, and good to have in the team. He wasn't going to be World Champion, but he was within two or three seconds of Senna everywhere we went. We could have done a lot worse than that.'

One of Dumfries's prime roles was to develop a new six-speed gearbox with Hewland internals within a Lotus-designed casing while Senna opted for the greater reliability of the proven five-speed unit. Reliability problems with the transmission certainly blunted Dumfries's track running and his end-of-season tally of three championship points does not truly reflect his ability. Ironically, the six-speed gearbox became an integral part of the Honda-powered

Lotus 99T, but with the Honda deal came Satoru Nakajima as second driver, so Dumfries's time with Team Lotus – and in Formula 1 – lasted just that one season.

In addition to a period running an active-suspension test programme for Benetton, Dumfries moved to endurance sports car racing, with Ecurie Ecosse, Sauber, Toyota and various Porsche teams. The biggest victory of his career came when he won the 1988 Le Mans 24 Hours driving a Jaguar XJR-9 for Tom Walkinshaw's Silk Cut Jaguar Team. In 1991 he elected to retire and, aside from briefly running a historic motorsport festival in the grounds of the ancestral seat of Mount Stuart House on the Isle of Bute, he has kept himself busy away from the sport ever since.

BELOW Johnny Dumfries was part of the 'Brit Pack' of 1986: from left, Jonathan Palmer, Dumfries, Nigel Mansell and Martin Brundle. *(John Townsend, F1 Pictures)*

Prix, brought Senna his third successive pole position but this time no victory. Both Senna and Dumfries were early retirements following failure of rear wheel bearings. There was little consolation in the fact that Senna's prime championship rival was also a non-finisher: Mansell's Honda engine misfired its way to retirement, leaving Prost to take the chequered flag for McLaren on a bone-dry fuel tank, just ahead of Piquet's Williams.

The fourth championship round, in Monaco, demonstrated that the Lotus 98T was not as invulnerable in qualifying as its rivals believed, although traffic was the main reason for Senna's relegation to third place behind Prost's McLaren and Mansell's Williams. Senna had in fact topped the time sheets in the first qualifying session, only to catch slower cars on every attempt as track conditions improved in the second session. While Mansell's lap was a

typical case of bravado, Prost, 'The Professor', produced a classic example of strategic thinking. Prost and his McLaren engineers had devised a chassis set-up that was easy on its tyres, allowing him to circulate for up to four laps (instead of the normal three-lap qualifying run) before finding a gap in the traffic and nailing the perfect lap.

Meanwhile, for Dumfries there was an embarrassing failure to qualify, although there were mitigating circumstances. A clash with the barriers robbed the rookie of valuable experience, then a differential failure ended his first qualifying attempt prematurely. In the final session he struggled with the six-speed gearbox and as a result was classified 24th, missing the cut as just 20 starters were allowed on the confined track.

In the race itself, Senna belied the wisdom that passing is impossible at Monaco by nipping ahead of Mansell on the opening lap on the run from Ste Devote to Casino Square. However, even Ayrton was unable to match the overtaking performance of Rosberg, who charged through the field in the second McLaren from ninth on the grid and grabbed second place as Senna made his mid-race tyre stop. The McLaren's combination of pace and lower tyre wear added up to a 1–2 for Prost and Rosberg, with Senna a frustrated third, his woes exacerbated by the fact that the result moved Prost ahead of him into the lead of the Drivers' Championship.

Subdued Spa

There was a subdued atmosphere at the Belgian Grand Prix, following the death a week earlier of former Team Lotus driver Elio de Angelis in a testing accident. Senna was again thwarted for pole position, forced to settle for fourth behind Piquet's Williams, a heroic Gerhard Berger in the low-downforce, low-drag Benetton-BMW, and Prost's McLaren. While one reason for the poor start position was that Senna's car had jumped out of gear three times on his fastest lap, it was also accepted that the Lotus 98T's high levels of downforce were being achieved at the expense of increased drag on Spa's ultra-long straights.

In the race itself, Senna created controversy by diving around the outside of Berger to grab second place at the first corner, the tight

La Source hairpin. That in turn triggered a collision between Berger and Prost, who then hit the inside barrier. As Senna carried on in his pursuit of Piquet, the prime beneficiary was Mansell, whose Williams had started fifth. He picked his way through the chaos and rapidly closed on Senna.

Ahead of them both, Piquet's Williams-Honda was drawing out a big lead – too big it would transpire. An electronics fault had left the Honda on full turbo boost and having all but drained his fuel tank in just 16 laps of the 43, Piquet had no option but to retire. Mansell, in contrast, was using his boost control to full advantage, running with the minimum possible to push Senna, then using a devastating burst of speed to vault into the lead during the round of mid-race tyre stops.

Team Lotus was powerless to prevent Mansell's first win of the 1986 season. In

ABOVE The Lotus 98T proved to be at its best on long, sweeping corners where its downforce provided exceptional speed. *(John Townsend, F1 Pictures)*

ABOVE In 1986 there was to be no repeat of Senna's Spa success the previous year; driving for fuel economy, he finished second. *(John Townsend, F1 Pictures)*

LEFT Johnny Dumfries was thwarted at Spa by a radiator problem, necessitating retirement. *(John Townsend, F1 Pictures)*

DEPART **Labatt** ARRIVÉE

ABOVE The Canadian Grand Prix demonstrated the Lotus 98T's Achilles' heel. Fuel consumption concerns saw Senna drop from second at the start to fifth by the finish. *(John Townsend, F1 Pictures)*

addition to the greater thirst of the Renault engine, the extra drag of the 98T also affected fuel consumption. In addition, as a result of the wheel-bearing troubles at Imola, the team had reverted to 1985-style rear suspension. This meant that hydraulic ride control, fitted in earlier races, could not be used, with a resulting loss of chassis balance and aerodynamic efficiency. Even the fitting of vertical aerofoils (the first barge boards?) behind the front wings only barely mitigated the difficulties.

In addition to Senna being forced to settle for second place, the handling imbalance perhaps also contributed to Dumfries failing to finish. After qualifying 13th and looking good for a top-ten finish, he spun at the fast Stavelot corner and retired after a stone had punched a hole in one of the car's radiators.

Mixed fortunes

The two consecutive North American races brought mixed fortunes for Team Lotus. In Canada, despite Senna's car being fitted with the later-specification rear suspension, the

Brazilian was pipped in qualifying by Mansell's Williams, which again used the relative economy of its Honda power unit to win the race. Senna could only manage fifth place, while Dumfries was eliminated after being rear-ended by Stefan Johansson's Ferrari.

In Detroit the team's luck changed, with Senna emphatically in control on the streets of Motown. His lap for pole position was over half a second faster than those of Mansell and Piquet, second and third in their Williams-Hondas. Come the race, Senna led initially before Mansell, on softer-compound tyres, demoted him to second. Unperturbed, Senna then waited until Mansell began to struggle with both tyres and brakes, and regained the lead.

Then it could all have so easily gone wrong for the Brazilian. On lap 12 the Lotus began to lose time with a slow puncture. Despite the resultant pit-stop taking just 12 seconds, so closely packed was the field that Senna rejoined eighth, but he was unbeatable in a race of attrition that saw his championship rivals falter, Piquet crashing out and Mansell, hobbled by glazed brakes,

FAR LEFT Senna dominated the 1986 United States Grand Prix in Detroit with pole position and victory. (John Townsend, F1 Pictures)

LEFT Detroit brought the second of Senna's two victories in 1986. (John Townsend, F1 Pictures)

BELOW Even the maestro overstepped the mark on occasion. The 1986 French Grand Prix at Paul Ricard saw Senna crash at Signes corner for the second successive year. (John Townsend, F1 Pictures)

finishing a lap down. Senna won by 31 seconds from Ligier-Renault driver Jacques Laffite, with Prost third, a result that put Ayrton back into the lead of the World Championship.

Despite having qualified a lowly 14th after another failure of the six-speed gearbox, Dumfries claimed seventh place, the best result of his Formula 1 career so far.

The next round, the French Grand Prix at Paul Ricard, was a rare case of lightning striking twice. Once again Senna claimed pole from Mansell and Piquet, taking advantage of a new Renault EF15C engine with reprofiled cylinder heads to boost power and smaller wastegates to aid throttle response. However, the race went badly. Senna was beaten off the line by Mansell, then, pushing hard to balance fuel consumption while keeping the Williams in sight, crashed off the track after hitting oil dropped by the Minardi of Andrea de Cesaris. This happened at Signes corner in precisely the same location and circumstances as the previous year. Mansell won the race from Prost, putting both back ahead of Senna in the World Championship

standings. To compound the disappointment, Dumfries, who had qualified 12th, retired after engine failure.

The British Grand Prix at Brands Hatch saw Williams dominant again with Piquet on pole and Mansell second, while Senna was third. The race was marred by a first-corner accident

in which popular Frenchman Jacques Laffite suffered leg injuries that ended his Formula 1 career. At the restart Mansell headed Piquet for a Williams 1–2, taking the championship lead. Senna retired with gearbox failure while Dumfries finished seventh.

The German Grand Prix at the ultra-fast Hockenheim circuit clearly favoured the TAG Turbo-powered McLarens with Rosberg and Prost 1–2 in qualifying, Senna again third. However, in another race that hinged on fuel consumption, the Williams-Hondas were the main opposition and Piquet won, with Senna second ahead of Mansell. Prost had been set to finish third, but his car ran out of fuel on the finishing straight of the last lap and, despite his best efforts to push it to the finish, was classified a lap down in sixth. Even Senna only reached the finish line with frantic weaving, to allow the fuel pumps to suck up the last dregs in the tank.

Title shoot-out

The first-ever Hungarian Grand Prix on the tight, twisting Hungaroring near Budapest saw another Senna pole. It was followed by a spectacular battle with Piquet, which saw the Williams driver claim victory from Senna and Mansell. This meant that there was now a four-

way battle for the title between Mansell, Prost, Senna and Piquet. Johnny Dumfries meanwhile achieved a career-best fifth place.

The Lotus 98T again proved ill-suited to the Österreichring in Austria. This fast, low-downforce track masked the poor throttle response of the BMW engines in the Benettons and emphasised their raw power, allowing Teo Fabi and Gerhard Berger to achieve a 1–2 in qualifying, with Senna only eighth. The race itself saw Prost take victory while Senna and Dumfries both retired with engine failure. The only redeeming feature of the weekend for Team Lotus was that both Williams-Hondas retired too.

It was a similar story for the Italian Grand Prix at Monza, where Fabi's Benetton took pole position from Prost and Mansell, with Ayrton fifth. Senna's car then broke its gearbox at the start and Dumfries suffered a similar failure on lap 18. Piquet hunted down team-mate Mansell to take the victory, putting the Williams drivers 1–2 in the World Championship.

The Portuguese Grand Prix had moved to a hot and dry late-summer date to avoid the spring rain that had marked Senna's first victory the previous year. Senna again claimed pole position, from Mansell and Prost, but right from the start of the race Mansell was in a class of his own, sailing with seeming impunity to victory

by an 18-second margin from Prost. Senna looked set to claim third only for his engine to stutter on the last lap, out of fuel despite fuel data indicating a further lap in the tank. As the Lotus slowed, Piquet passed for third place and, with it, the Constructors' title for Williams. Senna's fourth place, meanwhile, dropped him out of World Championship contention with two rounds remaining.

The Mexican Grand Prix saw Senna in the Lotus 98T claim his eighth pole position of the season, ahead of the Williams cars of Piquet and Mansell. The British driver provided start-line drama when he was unable to select first gear and, as he struggled off the line in second gear, somehow the rest of the field avoided contact as they swamped him, leaving him dead last. Piquet snatched the lead at the first corner and initially the race looked set to be a straight fight between him, Senna and Prost, whose McLaren's race pace was superior to that of the Lotus. During the race, however, the more durable Pirelli tyres fitted to Berger's Benetton-BMW allowed the Austrian to complete the race without a pit-stop and he duly won. In contrast, the fortunes of the Goodyear-shod drivers fluctuated as their tyres struggled with the temperature and abrasive track surface. After rounds of pit-stops, the

final order behind Berger wound up as Prost second, Senna third, Piquet fourth and Mansell fifth, leaving the Drivers' Championship wide open to the final round.

Swansong

It had been becoming clear that the last race of the season, the Australian Grand Prix in Adelaide, was going to be the end of an era. For 1987 a mandatory pop-off valve would restrict turbo boost to 4.0 bar, thus limiting engine power, as part of a two-year plan to phase out turbos in Formula 1. The Australian race was also the last for the Renault turbo

ABOVE Senna and the Lotus 98T were peerless in qualifying, claiming eight pole positions during 1986. *(John Townsend, F1 Pictures)*

BELOW In Mexico, Senna led from his eighth pole position, but he was destined to finish third. *(John Townsend, F1 Pictures)*

engine, as Renault had elected to withdraw from Formula 1.

Team Lotus had already struck a deal, partly brokered by Senna, for Honda to supply them with power units for 1987. As part of the deal, Senna would have a new team-mate, Japanese driver Satoru Nakajima. The Adelaide race would therefore be Johnny Dumfries's last. What was not generally known was that John Player Special sponsorship was also about to cease, marking the end for the famous black and gold colours.

Renault was determined to make its departure in style. The factory at Viry-Châtillon provided Senna's Lotus 98T with its ultimate EF15C qualifying engine. An evolution of the unit that had provided Senna with his final two pole positions in Portugal and Mexico, this version had still bigger turbochargers. To this day it remains unknown just how much power it generated as Renault's dynamometers were

'only' calibrated to around 1,100bhp, which the new engine reached a few hundred revs short of its 13,000rpm limit. It has been speculated that this ultimate engine developed something in excess of 1,300bhp from its diminutive 1,500cc.

In his report at the time, journalist Maurice Hamilton described Senna's final qualifying laps as a 'sight to behold'. Senna, wrote Hamilton, 'was hurling the Lotus around in great opposite-lock slides as if it was a tiny F3 machine, a virtuoso display of car control which was a rare privilege to witness.'

Senna was to be thwarted. In the latter stages of his all-out qualifying lap, yellow flags were waved for an expiring Zakspeed and a Tyrrell, and Senna had to lift. His lap time was only third fastest, half a second slower than the Williams-Hondas of Mansell and Piquet, who were in a three-way fight for the title with Prost, who was fourth on the grid.

At the race start, Senna grabbed the early lead from Mansell, but then was demoted by Piquet, all on the first lap! Senna's race was set to end with engine failure on lap 44, but the race will always be remembered for the demise of Mansell's championship hopes when his left-rear tyre exploded on the main straight at over 180mph. The Williams team then elected to call in Piquet for a precautionary tyre change, allowing Prost to take victory and win his second World Championship title.

Overshadowed by the dramas, an unsung success came from Dumfries. From 14th on the grid, he raced to a strong sixth place, gaining the privilege of being the last-ever JPS driver to take the chequered flag in a Formula 1 grand prix.

AFTERMATH: INNOVATION, THEN DECLINE

A new-look Team Lotus entered the 1987 season with high hopes and new bright yellow livery, courtesy of British American Tobacco's 'Camel' brand. In addition to Ayrton Senna's undoubted driving genius, the new Lotus-Honda 99T featured the same Honda V6 turbo engine as had been fitted to the previous season's front-running Williams cars, and there was a new secret weapon in the form of active suspension.

The active suspension system, which had been initially evaluated by the team in 1982 and 1983, continued to use pull-rod front and rear suspension assemblies, but the normal spring/damper units were replaced by hydraulic rams fed by a 3,000psi engine-driven hydraulic pump. Sensors and accelerometers mounted on and around the suspension arms supplied data to a small computer (located under the driver's seat) whose microprocessor signalled responses to the hydraulic rams.

In pre-season testing Senna enthusiastically rose to the challenge of developing this new technology, turning down the offer of a conventionally sprung fallback car with the words, 'Let's not waste time in the past; I will only drive active.' However, there was little doubt that the new technology pushed the team to its limits.

While designer Gérard Ducarouge dismissed the power loss from driving the hydraulics, around 12bhp, as 'inconsequential' given the Honda engine's 900bhp+ output, the system and its associated wiring and pipework added around 20kg (45lbs) to the car's weight. Adding further to the challenge was the need to design the new car around a power unit that was bulkier than the previous Renault engine.

In addition Team Lotus engineers also had to enter a new 'digital' era. Traditional data such as spring rates and wing angles were now all mathematical algorithms that had to be handled by computer. By the end of the 1987 season, the active suspension unit was calculated to have been making over 250 million 'decisions' per race.

Given the challenges, it is remarkable that the new car was successful from the outset. The opening race in Brazil saw Senna qualify third and briefly lead before retiring from second place with engine failure. His rookie team-mate, Satoru Nakajima, brought his car home

ABOVE **While fast and powerful, the Lotus 99T still suffered aerodynamic shortcomings compared with its rivals.** *(John Townsend, F1 Pictures)*

BELOW **Ayrton Senna was the driving force in uniting Honda and Team Lotus.** *(John Townsend, F1 Pictures)*

seventh, the first of a series of top-ten finishes that gained the Japanese driver increasing respect as much more than a mere Honda-sponsored 'shoe-in'.

The Lotus 99T and its active suspension made history in qualifying for the San Marino Grand Prix when Senna claimed the first-ever pole position for an active suspension car, eventually coming home second to the Williams-Honda of Nigel Mansell. On the bumpy and twisting street circuits of Monaco and Detroit the car was in a class of its own, Senna claiming back-to-back race victories.

However, the Lotus 99T was not as good an all-round package as the conventionally suspended Williams-Honda cars, whose aerodynamic efficiency was clearly superior. This manifested itself not only in better straight-line speed but also in fuel efficiency. In order to generate similar downforce, the Lotus wing settings generated greater drag, which in turn meant Senna would frequently have to reduce boost settings to reach the chequered flag while Williams drivers Mansell and Piquet, in similarly powered cars, battled wheel to wheel for the title ahead of him.

Brazilian switch

At the start of the 1988 season Senna was gone, moving to a newly Honda-powered McLaren for the final season of the turbocharged Formula 1 era. Replacing him at Team Lotus came reigning World Champion Nelson Piquet. Both he and Nakajima would drive the Lotus-Honda 100T, an evolution of the previous year's car with conventional suspension.

The reason for the abandonment of active suspension was a change in engine regulations. With a mandated reduction in turbo boost from 4.0 bar to 2.5 bar, power dropped from around 900bhp to 600bhp, which meant that the further loss of power to run the active system – thought to be about 5% – simply was not viable. The new car, therefore, reverted to springs and shock absorbers.

The 1989 season will be remembered for the mighty battle between the two McLaren drivers who dominated the season. Senna achieved his first World Championship title with eight wins to Prost's seven, while McLaren set a record for most races won in a season. The only other winner in

the 16-race season was Gerhard Berger, driving for Ferrari, while the best Piquet could manage in the Lotus was third place in three races.

Late in the season Ducarouge at last discovered the reason why the Lotus had more drag than rival cars. Checks revealed a disparity in results between two comparable wind tunnels, meaning that vital aerodynamic data had been skewed. The findings came too late to save the season, or Ducarouge's job, and the Frenchman was replaced as chief designer by ex-Williams aerodynamicist Frank Dernie.

A new era – and a showdown

The start of a new 3.5-litre normally aspirated era in 1989 saw Team Lotus without Honda power as the Japanese manufacturer chose to focus on McLaren, while Renault opted to make its Formula 1 return with Williams. A customer Judd V8, which inevitably lacked the development budget of the rival engines from big manufacturers, therefore powered the Lotus 101.

With no points scored by Team Lotus in the first five races, a management showdown occurred at the British Grand Prix at Silverstone. The Chapman family, who were still the main shareholders in Team Lotus International, persuaded Peter Warr and chairman Fred Bushell to resign. Tony Rudd, who was at the time working for Group Lotus, was appointed executive chairman and Rupert Mainwaring team manager, but little could be done to improve results.

Straitened times

After Camel moved its sponsorship elsewhere, straitened finances meant that the Lotus 102 chassis had to soldier on for three seasons, first with a Lamborghini V12 (1990), then a Judd EV V8 (1991) and finally a Ford-Cosworth HB V8 (1992). The driver line-up included Derek Warwick, Martin Donnelly (until a career-ending accident at Jerez), Johnny Herbert, Julian Bailey and Mika Häkkinen (a future double World Champion), but at best the cars were only midfield runners.

Former Benetton team manager Peter Collins and Team Lotus chief engineer Peter Wright headed a consortium that bought the team from the Chapman family in 1991. Despite a continuing lack of funding, a final ray of hope arrived midway into the 1992 season when the Lotus 107 appeared. Powered by the ubiquitous Ford HB, the car scored a succession of fourth places that year and into 1993, and then in early 1994 an updated version powered by a Mugen-Honda V10 engine raced with less success. It and a shorter-wheelbase variant, the Lotus 109, truly marked the end of an era when Team Lotus closed its doors at the end of the 1994 season.

Chapter Three

Anatomy of the Lotus 97T and 98T

The definitive JPS Lotus-Renault Formula 1 cars, the Lotus 97T and 98T, followed a steady line of evolution from designer Gérard Ducarouge's first complete design for Team Lotus, the 95T of 1984. In this chapter the components of the 97T and 98T are explained in detail, along with descriptions of the way in which all of the cars' assemblies and systems work and how they evolved.

OPPOSITE The cockpit of Lotus 98T/4, the last Lotus-Renault to be built, remains exactly as it was when Ayrton Senna drove the car during the second half of the 1986 season. *(James Ward)*

Roy Scorer's cutaway shows what lies beneath the skin of the Lotus 98T.

(Roy Scorer)

1 Front wheel
2 Front wing
3 Front suspension
4 LED and LCD driver display
5 Alcantara suede-covered steering wheel
6 Manual gearshift knob
7 Steel roll-over hoop
8 Engine electronic control unit
9 Fuel cell in monocoque
10 Fuel/air plenum chamber
11 Renault EF15 engine
12 Periscope air scoop for turbo inlet
13 Rear wing endplate
14 Adjustable rear wing element
15 Exhaust-fed rear diffuser
16 Rear suspension
17 Damper with pneumatic ride-height control
18 Carbon-carbon disc brakes
19 Quick-removal wheel nut
20 Turbocharger
21 Air-to-air intercooler
22 Sidepod-mounted radiator

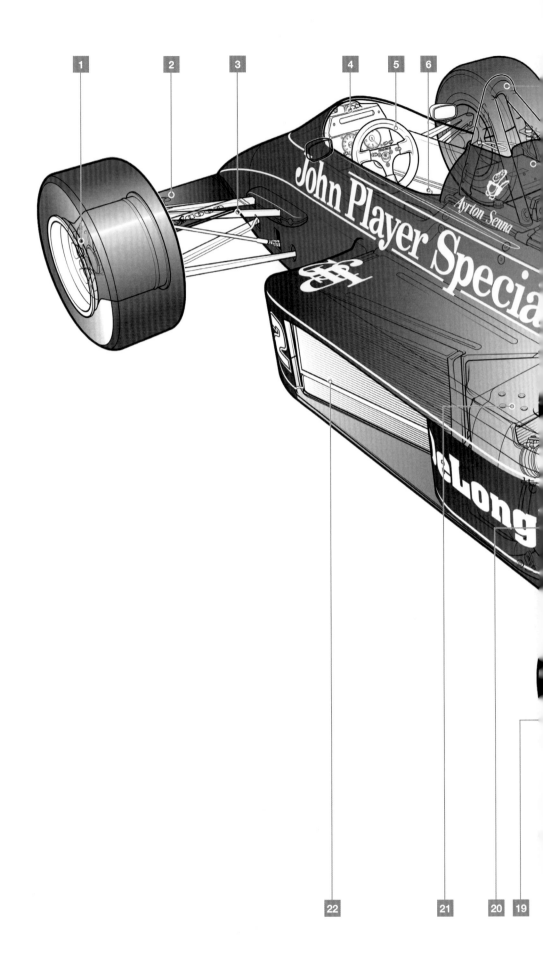

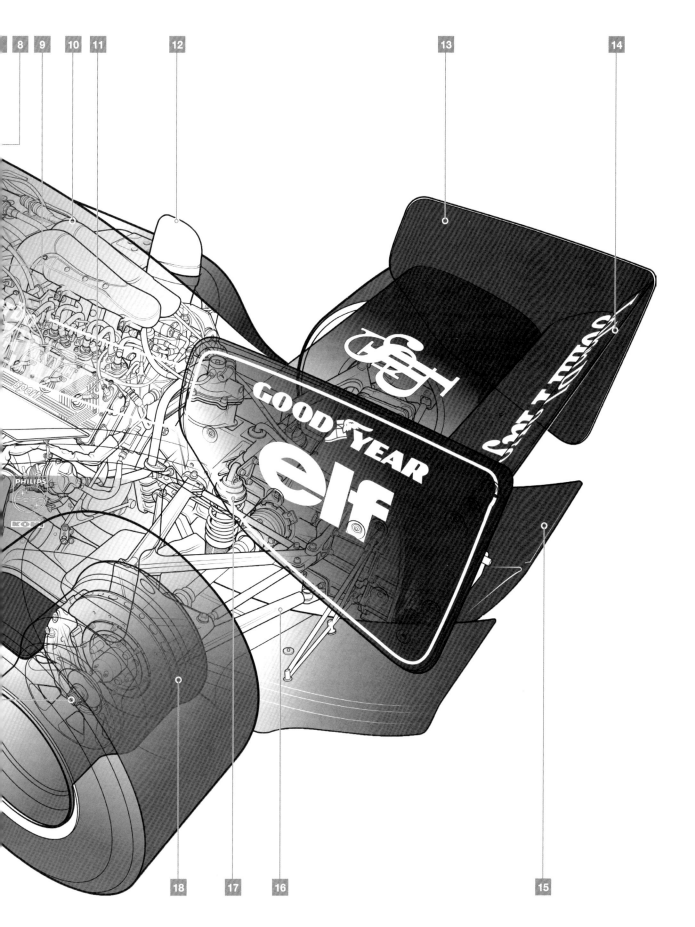

8 9 10 11 12 13 14

18 17 16 15

These beautiful studio views of Lotus 98T/4, Senna's race car for the second half of the 1986 season, show the car in all its majesty. In markets where tobacco advertising was banned, the car would carry victory laurels celebrating Team Lotus's seven world championships instead of the John Player Special lettering, as reproduced here (bottom left photograph) on Lotus 98T/4. *(James Ward)*

Design and development

All aspects of design, development, pattern-
making and construction were carried
out in-house at the team's base in the stately
surroundings of Ketteringham Hall near Hethel
in Norfolk, with prototype design taking place in
'The Chapel', the top-secret drawing office. The
team later developed a secured-access special
prototyping area to allow developments to
continue away from prying eyes, while detailed
suspension design and chassis design was
carried out in the main drawing office.

Design work on each successive car would
begin late in the previous season, with the
aim of having the first complete car ready in
February for a pre-season shakedown, often
combined with a sponsor photo-session at
either Hethel or a UK track such as Donington
Park. The more extensive pre-season testing of
the new car would then move to circuits with

more favourable weather, including Kyalami in
South Africa, Paul Ricard in southern France
and Rio de Janeiro in Brazil.

Team Lotus mechanic Chris Dinnage would
spend much of the 'closed' season helping to
build the prototype car, before moving on to
work on the successive race and 'spare' cars.
Once the respective seasons began, he then
took over responsibility for running the team's
spare cars.

'Prototype building started with a wooden
chassis buck,' says Dinnage. 'Then the content
was built around that. Pipework, plumbing and
wiring looms were schemed rather than drawn,
to allow more flexibility as the car developed.
In particular with the early turbo cars, it was
almost *ad hoc* where the various pipes and
intercoolers would fit.'

The first chassis, 01, was used for these
tests with any changes or refinements being
passed back to chassis 02 and 03, which would

become the principal race cars. Chassis 01 would then serve as the team's first spare car, to be joined by another spare, 04, by the time the World Championship arrived in Europe. In the case of the Lotus 97T and 98T (as with the 95T), just four examples of each type were built.

Construction

The Lotus 97T continued the basic design and aerodynamics established by the 95T, and indeed Team Lotus cars of the previous decade. The cars featured a carbon-composite monocoque 'tub' along with a stressed engine and gearbox combination, acting as the mounting points for the rear suspension and aerodynamic aids.

Despite being derived from the 95T, the 97T for the 1985 season was a brand-new car with no interchangeable parts. While earlier 'carbon-tub' cars in effect merely

substituted carbon-composite components for aluminium structures, during the 1985 and 1986 seasons the 97T and 98T featured new refinements as Team Lotus pushed the limits of carbon/Kevlar-composite moulding in monocoque construction.

It should be remembered that the first use of monocoque construction for a grand prix car was by Team Lotus, when Colin Chapman utilised a lightweight riveted aluminium structure instead of a tubular spaceframe in his Lotus 25 of 1962. While the McLaren MP4/1C became the first car to race with a moulded carbonfibre monocoque, in 1983, research work was already underway in parallel at Team Lotus. While McLaren subcontracted its early production to Hercules Aerospace in the USA, Lotus opted from the outset to build its monocoques in-house.

Despite having relatively small premises devoted to the new technology, little more

ABOVE With bodywork removed, the carbonfibre/ Kevlar monocoque construction of the Lotus 98T can be seen, with aluminium studs delineating the position of integral load-bearing aluminium bulkheads. *(James Ward)*

than a large garage in the stable block at Ketteringham Hall next to the main workshops, Team Lotus was at the forefront of carbon-composite construction at this time, experimenting with moulding different 'weaves' of the core material and various lay-up techniques. The prime materials were woven carbonfibre cloth and DuPont Corporation's patent Kevlar aramid, both of which offer exceptional stiffness and tensile strength, with the stiffer carbonfibre being complemented by the higher impact resistance and kinetic energy absorption of Kevlar, which also costs less.

One specific characteristic of carbon materials is that their strength is directional, as loads can only be transmitted along the length of the fibres. The strength and malleability of the material can therefore be controlled by the use of different weaves. At one end of the range is unidirectional cloth, in which 90% or more of the fibres run in one direction with the remaining

ABOVE This view of 98T/4 with all bodywork removed provides a magnificent study of the car's monocoque structure and carefully packaged systems, which include side-exiting radiators for improved aerodynamic performance. The carbon chassis carried sponsor logos, ensuring exposure even when the bodywork was removed. *(James Ward)*

fibres merely providing integrity until the bonding process is activated. The most commonly utilised version is 50/50 cloth, with the fibres equally woven at right angles, allowing loads to be distributed across the weave.

The majority of these materials were supplied to Team Lotus as 'pre-preg' sheets of woven material already impregnated with epoxy resin, allowing the composites to be cut, moulded and shaped before being bonded. Although epoxy bonding resins weigh significantly more than the carbon and do not further add to the strength, they play an important role in forming the matrix securing the fibres and preventing movement

OPPOSITE A triple-element wing, centrally supported, and exhaust-blown diffuser dominate the rear of the 98T. *(James Ward)*

Described as the architect of the JPS Lotus Renault success, Gérard Ducarouge combined a racing philosophy with a strict engineering methodology and a dash of Gallic flair and intuition to create not only a string of successful JPS-Lotus cars but also some other effective Formula 1 cars of the 1970s and 1980s. His arrival at Team Lotus in 1984 galvanised the team into one of its most innovative periods.

RIGHT Gérard Ducarouge was rarely without his trademark sunglasses, whatever the weather. *(John Townsend, F1 Pictures)*

BELOW Gérard Ducarouge and Elio de Angelis. *(John Townsend, F1 Pictures)*

Like many in the field, Ducarouge honed his skills in the aerospace industry of the early 1960s. He gained his *Degré Supérieur* at the École Nationale Technique d'Aéronautique in Toulouse, one of the most prestigious and selective *grandes écoles* in France, before joining the Nord Aviation company in 1964 to work on missile projects.

In 1965 Ducarouge moved to another aerospace company, Matra, to work in its newly formed motorsport division and he rose rapidly through the organisation. After involvement with Matra's Formula 3 and Formula 2 cars, he designed the Cosworth-powered Matra MS10 and MS80 Formula 1 cars, the latter winning the 1969 World Championship with Jackie Stewart. Ducarouge then masterminded Matra's sports car designs, which scored a hat-trick of victories at Le Mans in 1972, 1973 and 1974. For the 1976 season he joined Guy Ligier's new Formula 1 team, which had acquired Matra's Formula 1 assets, including its V12 engine.

Ducarouge's creative design was exemplified by the JS5, the first Formula 1 Ligier, famous for its distinctive 'teapot' airbox design used in the first few races of 1976. Later that year Jacques Laffite took pole position for the Italian Grand Prix, and into 1977, at the Swedish Grand Prix, he gave Ligier its first victory. Success continued with the Ligier JS11, which dominated the first half of the 1979 World Championship in the hands of Laffite and Patrick Depailler, only later being overhauled by eventual champions Jody Scheckter and Ferrari.

Ducarouge's mercurial temperament later led to a clash with Guy Ligier and in 1981 he moved to Alfa Romeo. His sojourn there was brief as another flare-up led to his dismissal in April 1983 at the French Grand Prix.

On becoming aware of Ducarouge's availability, Peter Warr moved quickly to secure his services for Team Lotus, drafting him in alongside Lotus 93T designer Martin Ogilvie to reverse the disappointing form of the first Renault turbo cars. Despite Ducarouge's reputation for egotism, it says a great deal about both designers that they successfully worked together to initiate 'a whirlwind programme of change'.

It is now legend that under Ducarouge's leadership Team Lotus, using the 'obsolete' tubs from previous DFV-powered cars, created the all-new Renault turbo-powered Lotus 94T in time for Elio de Angelis and Nigel Mansell to race competitively at their sponsor's most important race, the British Grand Prix.

Ducarouge's successive designs, the 95T, 97T and 98T, all pushed the boundaries of technology in carbon structures, aerodynamics and mechanical engineering. Equally important was Ducarouge's relationship with the team's highest-profile driver. Neither he nor Ayrton Senna suffered fools gladly (if at all) but they developed a close bond and mutual trust in one another's judgement.

This was perhaps best illustrated in the year after the final Lotus-Renault car was raced. Ducarouge proposed all-active, computer-controlled hydropneumatic suspension for the Lotus-Honda 99T and convinced Senna that, despite gloomy predictions elsewhere, it would work. He was, of course, correct, as demonstrated by Senna's final victory for Team Lotus at that year's Detroit Grand Prix.

By 1988 Team Lotus was increasingly cash-strapped and Ducarouge left to go first to Lola and then Larrousse before returning to Matra to help develop the spectacular F1-powered Renault Espace demonstration 'Formula 1' vehicle. He later suffered long-term illness and passed away at the age of 72 on 19 February 2015.

Always stylish and frequently outspoken, Ducarouge had a powerful motivational presence, whether in the paddock or the workshop. He also had a charming, wry sense of humour and was the first to see the joke when, at the end of the 1986 season, Renault executives made a presentation to him in commemoration of their four years of working with Team Lotus. Ducarouge was solemnly presented with 16 packets of cigarettes, each one carrying the date and venue of the following season's races. It was a quiet comment on his habit of scrounging cigarettes from all and sundry in the pitlane and paddock!

and crack propagation. Bonding takes place in an autoclave, a high-pressure, high-temperature oven; Team Lotus had several autoclaves, the largest of which could accommodate a complete Formula 1 monocoque.

Throughout the process, cleanliness is critical as grease or dust can prevent the epoxy and the composites bonding correctly, reducing strength. Composite production was therefore carried out in conditions akin to an operating theatre, with personnel wearing disposable overalls and gloves, while air-filtration systems extracted any noxious fumes and minimised the ingress of dust.

The finished carbon/Kevlar structure was estimated to be around 70% stiffer than an equivalent aluminium design and almost 25% lighter. This combination of high strength and lightness allowed the complete car to weigh rather less than the 540kg minimum specified by the regulations. It is beneficial to make a Formula 1 car underweight, as the ballast required to reach the minimum weight can be positioned in locations that aid the car's centre of gravity, weight distribution, handling and traction.

During the lay-up process, the void in the sandwich between the two layers of the car's carbon and Kevlar composite monocoque was filled with a Nomex and paper foil material during the early days, but for the 97T and 98T chassis an aluminium-foil honeycomb material, initially developed for use in Matra rockets, was used. Ducarouge had initially planned to use this construction technique to increase crash protection in the stillborn Lotus 96 Indycar against the concrete walls of banked oval tracks in the USA, but he then realised that this new construction method could make a Formula 1 monocoque both stronger and more rigid, with little or no weight penalty.

Most of Team Lotus's composite monocoques were produced using what was known as the 'cigarette-pack' construction technique – ironic given the team's major sponsor. As in a multi-piece cardboard cigarette pack, the monocoque contained a succession of folded panels made up of two carbon-composite skins to form upper and lower halves of a shell-like structure. Prior to these being bonded together and hardened in an autoclave, structural bulkheads machined from solid

RIGHT Prior to the 98T, earlier Lotus carbon-composite tubs used 'cigarette packet' construction, with a succession of folded panels bonded together. *(Classic Team Lotus)*

BELOW The Lotus 98T used a single-piece moulding for lighter weight and greater rigidity. *(Author)*

aluminium billets were inserted at key 'hard points' to carry components and transmit loads into the structure.

For the 1986 season, this construction method was refined for the definitive Lotus-Renault 98T. The machined aluminium bulkheads were inserted in the mould at the laying-up process, allowing the tub to be moulded as a single unified unit, making the finished monocoque even lighter, yet still more rigid.

Chassis

The carbon/Kevlar composite monocoque extends from the car's angular, wedge-shaped nose, with a tapering, flat-sided, rhomboidal scuttle structure carrying the mounting points for the front suspension wishbones and pull-rod units. Rearwards, the monocoque continues to taper until about

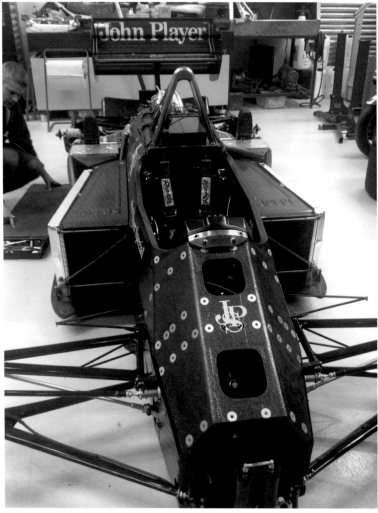

the driver's shoulders in the cockpit area, before running with parallel sides to form the foundation for the fuel tank, chromed steel tubular roll hoop (behind the driver's head), radiators and sidepods.

Mandated for the first time in 1985 and evaluated by Formula 1's first crash tests, a deformable nose section provides impact protection ahead of the 'hard' pedal box protecting the driver's feet. Starting at the front, the first of the aluminium bulkheads within the composite monocoque structure carries the attachment for the forward arm of the lower suspension wishbone and forms the front end of the pedal box. Behind it a 'scuttle' bulkhead forms the rear of the pedal box as well as carrying upper suspension mounts, inboard dampers, steering rack and anti-roll bar. Next, the 'dash bulkhead' carries the rearward arm of the lower suspension wishbone, the instrument

displays and the first of the two mandated tubular steel roll-over bars.

The Fédération International du Sport Automobile (FISA) safety regulations of the era also required that the forward roll-over hoop, ahead of the driver, had to be at least as high as the steering wheel, to protect the driver's hands. A minimum distance of 500mm between the front and rear hoops effectively dictated the cockpit aperture length and the rules demanded that a line drawn between the tops of the hoops should pass above the driver's helmet. The rear roll hoop was mounted on the rearmost pair of aluminium bulkheads, which were positioned to the front and rear of the fuel tank, with the final bulkhead forming the firewall with the engine compartment.

One notable feature of the 97T and 98T was a revision in the airflow through the side-

BELOW **Rules required that the chassis has a flat floor, but the whole car was designed to optimise under-car aerodynamics.** *(James Ward)*

mounted radiators. In common with earlier Lotus-Renault cars, the cooling air entered the sidepods from inlet ducts behind the front wheels, but instead of expelling the air heated by the combined water/oil radiators via vents on the top of the sidepods, the 97T and 98T discharged to the side, where the heated air aided airflow around the rear tyres owing to its lower density. The smoother top profile of the sidepods also benefited aerodynamic efficiency around the rear of the car.

'Renault and Ferrari simultaneously appeared with them too, but it was our own idea,' said Ducarouge in an interview with Mike Lawrence, admitting that this development was not solely his own. 'Side venting provides better cooling and better aerodynamics. It clears the airflow to the rear wing.'

Inlet air for the turbochargers and 'intercoolers' was also carefully ducted within the sidepods in order to optimise thermal efficiency and fuel-charge density as well as, again, to use exhausted air to aid rear wing and diffuser aerodynamics.

While the front suspension is secured direct to the monocoque, the rear suspension pick-up points are located on the cast-magnesium gearbox casing, which, along with the engine, forms a stressed structure at the rear of the car. Six mounting bolts secure the transaxle, which incorporates both the gearbox and differential, to the engine. It in turn is bolted to a small spaceframe on the rear face of the monocoque

structure just behind the fuel tank and an 11-litre dry-sump oil tank that is also enclosed in the rearmost section of the monocoque. All fittings on the monocoque and associated chassis components are secured by copper-plated bolts with long, unthreaded shanks, requiring a zero-tolerance fit. All bolts were sized according to their specific purpose.

The fuel tank, a Kevlar-reinforced rubber fuel cell made by ATL (Aero Tec Laboratories), is contained within the monocoque between the driver and engine compartments.

The bottom of the chassis is completed by a removable carbonfibre 'flat floor', required to meet FISA's aerodynamic regulations, although its plan-form features a distinctive 'coke-bottle' profile to control air velocity and aid rear-end airflow. Titanium-steel skid plates prevent abrading of the structure when the car 'bottoms' over track undulations. Spectacular sparks from skid plates scraping the track were an integral part of the Formula 1 spectacle of the era.

A further innovative feature of the monocoque was that its natural matt-black, carbonfibre finish was enhanced by sponsor decals, ensuring brand exposure even when the car was in the pits with its bodywork removed. On the lower part of the tub the matt-black finish and decals remained visible even with the top bodywork fitted.

Bodywork

One Team Lotus characteristic dating back to the dawn of the John Player Special era was the use of a one-piece body section clothing the carbon/Kevlar monocoque. The bodywork incorporated the nose, cockpit surround, engine cover, the top of the radiator cover and sidepod. This long but ultra-light carbon/Kevlar structure could be lifted rapidly on or off the car by just two people in order to give access to all the key components. When off the car, this bodywork was normally placed on a pair of metal stands.

While the JPS Lotus 97T had separate bodywork side panels providing access hatches to the radiators, turbochargers and engine bay, for the 98T these were incorporated in the one-piece bodywork, allowing more rapid access to

BELOW The one-piece removable upper body was a Lotus characteristic.
(Classic Team Lotus)

RIGHT Earlier cars still retained separate side panels. *(John Townsend, F1 Pictures)*

CENTRE The Lotus 98T featured a fully removable upper body, aiding access to the turbochargers and wastegates. *(Author)*

the key areas. In particular this enabled easier access to facilitate quick changes of the red-hot turbochargers and wastegates by mechanics wearing heatproof gloves during full-boost qualifying sessions.

'The 97T wasn't a bad car to work on,' recalls Chris Dinnage, 'and in some respects it was the best car we ever built. The 98T, though, had some advantages, with better access and attention to detail. For qualifying with the 98T, we'd take off the wastegates – low compression, big turbos, maybe 5.5 bar boost, 1,200 horsepower. We'd change wheels, tyres – *and* turbos – during the qualifying sessions.'

A mandatory reduction in fuel tank size from 220 litres to 195 litres allowed the 98T to feature rear bodywork and an engine cover that was smoother in profile that its predecessor, with just a small hump to clear the Renault engine's bulky 'dromedary' plenum chamber on top of the engine. The smaller fuel tank also allowed the control unit for the Renault/Bendix 'Renix' electronic engine management system to be placed above the tank, just beneath the roll hoop, easing access and allowing a smaller, lighter wiring loom to be fitted.

Just beneath the rear roll hoop, a further neat touch on the 98T was a small water reservoir used during qualifying sessions to spray cool water into the turbocharger intercoolers, lowering the temperature of the fuel/air charge and increasing its density, thereby boosting horsepower. For the race, when ultimate boost was not required, a swift change of the pipework allowed the tank to be used as the driver's drinks bottle.

Contrary to immediate appearances, the Lotus 97T and 98T cars both have a

RIGHT Quick access to turbos and wastegates was critical during qualifying. *(John Townsend, F1 Pictures)*

windscreen, but the Perspex adjoining the carbon/Kevlar cockpit surround is so heavily tinted that it blends seamlessly into the car's overall black livery.

During the 1980s, tobacco advertising was becoming subject to restriction, and logos and brand names were banned in markets such as France and Germany. In these instances each Lotus raced instead with the letters TL (for Team Lotus) in a JPS-like typeface on its front wings, while the sides of the car carried, instead of the brand name, a series of laurel garlands bearing the dates of the team's Constructors' Championship victories (1963, 1965, 1968, 1970, 1972, 1973 and 1978).

Aerodynamics

Even with their prodigious horsepower, the turbocharged Formula 1 cars of the 1980s marked the start of the era in which aerodynamics began to dominate car design and performance. Team Lotus had traditionally been at the forefront of these developments with first Colin Chapman, then Martin Ogilvie, Gérard Ducarouge and Peter Wright all pushing the limits of available wind-tunnel and computational technology to match aerodynamic efficiency with downforce continuously through each racing season.

Both the Lotus 97T and the 98T represented this process of continuous evolution. They were initially conceptualised with aerodynamic development using 25%-scale models in a wind tunnel at Imperial College, London, then the full-size prototype car was tested in the 100%-scale wind tunnel at the Institut Aérotechnique at St Cyr near Paris.

Although an all-new design, the 97T carried forward the key principles established by its predecessor, the 95T. It featured a clean upper body surface to maximise smooth airflow from the low-mounted nose aerofoils, across the sidepods to the single, central post-mounted rear wing, while beneath it, under-car downforce was supplemented by a large exhaust-blown rear diffuser.

Typical of the in-season development by Team Lotus was the adoption midway through 1985 of 'periscope' turbocharger air inlets on the top rear of the sidepods of the 97T. These replaced low-profile slit vents in the surface, with the 'periscopes' using the car's airflow to add 'ram-air' to the pressure on the turbo inlets. These intakes were retained on the Lotus 98T for the 1986 season.

Front wings

Among the aerodynamic hallmarks of the 97T were its trapezoidal, tapering-chord nose wings. The shape was developed to maintain downforce while reducing drag by deflecting airflow and vortices along the sides of the bodywork. Constructed of carbon composite, they were left unpainted, with gold JPS and Goodyear sponsorship decals applied straight on to the matt-black finish.

Secured to the nose section by 'pip pins' to allow rapid removal and replacement, the horizontal sections of the wings were each made in two sections, with a larger, lower-incidence forward section supplemented by a smaller, adjustable-incidence rear flap, the angle of which could quickly be altered to balance the car's handling. A small gap between the two aerofoils played an important role in acting as an aerodynamic 'slot', accelerating airflow to enhance the wings' efficiency. On the outside edge of the front aerofoils, a shallow triangular endplate completed each wing unit.

The birth of barge boards

The Lotus 98T sported larger, squarer, tapered front-wing endplates and parallel-chord nose-wing elements, with a new aerodynamic aid directing airflow around the front wheels and sidepods. Located on brackets emanating from the radiator air intakes, a pair of 'turning vanes' was used on selected circuits to smooth airflow behind the front wheels and accelerate it around the leading edge of the sidepods, enhancing the low-pressure area under the car. In subsequent seasons this Team Lotus innovation was developed by many teams, creating the 'barge boards' along the lower cockpit sides that became a feature of almost every Formula 1 car of the 1990s and 2000s.

Rear wing

At the rear of both the Lotus 97T and 98T, the rear wing was another component that was the subject of constant evolution through the 1985 and 1986 seasons. While effectively appearing to be a single T-shaped assembly mounted on a central pillar with a pair of large, vertical endplates extending forward to the rear-axle line, the wing was principally made up in three sections with the pillar-mounted forward element featuring a selection of aerofoil sections with different thicknesses to suit the drag characteristics of different circuits.

The rear elements of the wing were made up of two aerofoil sections mounted via the endplates to offer full-width unbroken aerofoil elements across the width of the car. Adjustable for incidence, the elements were of progressively steeper angle to the airflow and, as with the front wings, the gaps between the

elements were carefully calculated to create aerodynamic 'slots' with the resulting venturi effect boosting airflow and wing efficiency.

A further feature shared by the front and rear wings is that their trailing edges feature a 'Gurney flap', a small lip extending the width of the wing almost perpendicular to the aerofoil surface. Conceived by former Indycar and grand prix driver Dan Gurney in the early 1970s, the lip increases pressure on the pressure side of the aerofoil, reducing aerodynamic 'curl-over' and helping the boundary layer of air to stay attached to the trailing edge.

At slower circuits requiring yet more rear downforce, at the potential expense of greater

BELOW Turning vanes, later known as barge boards, were an innovation, smoothing airflow along the sidepods. *(James Ward)*

BOTTOM For high-speed, low-downforce tracks such as Monza, a dual-element rather than triple-element wing would have been used. *(Author)*

RIGHT Both front and rear aerofoil angles were rapidly adjustable.
(Classic Team Lotus)

BELOW High-velocity exhaust gases created a 'boundary layer', increasing the effectiveness of the rear diffuser; rear-end and underfloor aerodynamic downforce were critical to harnessing the turbo horsepower.
(Author)

drag, additional lower wing elements could be added below the main planes, bolted at each end to the wing endplates. This was normally a single supplementary aerofoil, sited behind the rear wheels and generating downforce from airflow carried across the rear bodywork. Below it, meanwhile, a prominent rear diffuser extended from the rear of the floor, generating downforce both by air pressure on its top surface and by suction from the acceleration of air from underneath the car as it exited the rear.

Additional aerofoils were also used on the 97T in selected races, mounted just ahead of the rear wheels on the upper trailing edge of the sidepod. These were subsequently outlawed for the 1986 season by a new rule that banned the mounting of any rear aerodynamic devices ahead of the rear-axle line. The 98T thus had clean sidepod tops, with the exception of the 'periscope' turbocharger air intakes, and airflow around the rear wheels was managed via the use of deeper rear-wing endplates.

While the Lotus 97T and 98T pushed aerodynamic performance to the known limits of the era, they were not perfect. In low-drag, low-downforce trim at Monza, the 97T suffered from porpoising, created by movement of the centre of air pressure bearing down on the car. It was cured when the sideplates to the rear underbody were cut off, whereupon Senna qualified on pole position, and he went on to finish third in the race.

A bigger issue was aerodynamic efficiency. As a result of their wide tyres and aerodynamic devices optimised for ultimate downforce, all Formula 1 cars of the era had a drag co-efficient of between 1.0 and 1.5, in comparison with 0.35 to 0.5 for a typical road car. At Lotus, as with their rivals, work on aerodynamics prioritised downforce and grip far ahead of drag reduction.

Given the prodigious horsepower of the turbocharged engines, this high level of drag did not show itself in any lack of straight-line performance and the cars were routinely geared to achieve in excess of 200mph. As the 1985 and 1986 seasons went on, however, it was clear that teams such as McLaren and Williams were able to match the race pace of the Lotus cars with lower fuel consumption, despite the best efforts of Renault to develop more economical running profiles for the engines.

Only in 1987, when the new relationship with Honda gave Team Lotus access to the Honda-supported, 40%-scale, rolling-road wind tunnel at Imperial College, London, did it transpire that there was a mismatch between some of the data provided by the smaller wind tunnel at Imperial College and the full-size tunnel at the Institut Aérotechnique. As a result, the subsequent Lotus-Honda 99T featured some significant aerodynamic revisions to improve drag efficiency.

Under-car aerodynamics and blown diffuser

One of the most distinctive features of the rear of the Lotus 97T and 98T is the prominent low-mounted rear diffuser, a steeply curving carbonfibre structure extending from behind the engine and gearbox to the permitted 600mm limit behind the rear-axle line. The evolution of the

diffuser stemmed from the need to develop new means of regaining the downforce and cornering power lost after FISA, on safety grounds, banned the use of venturi tunnels creating suction from air flowing under a car's sidepods.

From the start of the 1983 season, the floor of a Formula 1 car had to be flat within the car's wheelbase and across the full width of the sidepods. At a stroke this reduced aerodynamic downforce levels by more than 50%, but by 1985 progress in generating traction from the airflow at the front and rear of the car, meant that lap times and cornering speeds were back to 1982 levels, and in some cases even beyond them.

The rear diffuser was one of the prime contributors to this surge in aerodynamic performance. The diffuser in effect accelerates the velocity of the underbody airflow, and as air pressure decreases with velocity (according to Bernoulli's principle) the pressure becomes lower below the car than above it, resulting in downforce. This effect is further enhanced by the close proximity of the airflow to the lower edges of the rear wing elements. By carefully managing the airflow of each unit in harmony with the next, even greater energy is created.

In the case of the Lotus 97T and 98T, Team Lotus aerodynamicists added another new dimension by routing the exhaust gases from the engine on to the diffuser, pre-empting by more than 20 years the exhaust-blown rear diffusers used by Brawn GP and Red Bull in their World Championship-winning success. As with the later cars, the blown gases do much more than merely add to and energise the airflow on the diffuser itself; the cars' exhausts are designed to fire a blade of hot air across the top of the diffuser, extending the boundary layer and preventing the airflow separating, which has the effect of extending the virtual effect of the top deck of the diffuser well beyond the limits of its physical dimensions.

Cockpit

The cockpit of the 97T and the 98T was designed to form part of the mandatory 'survival cell' and the requirements for impact protection included two key elements. First, there had to be dual roll-over bars (the forward one acting as the dashboard mounting) in specified positions, including the need for a minimum 500mm between them in order to allow a sufficiently large cockpit aperture for the driver to exit the car in no more than five seconds. Second, box-section members either side of the driver had to be at least 220mm high, cover at least 60% of the wheelbase, and extend 500mm ahead of the driver's feet.

The cockpit contains a mandatory life-support system that allowed the driver to breathe cold air in the event of a fire and a built-in fire extinguisher system with outlets in both the cockpit and the engine compartment.

The seat, moulded to the driver's form using polyurethane foam, is made of carbonfibre and screwed to the floor of the car, and a six-point safety harness is fitted. Unlike contemporary Formula 1 cars, with two-pedal controls and sequential gear selection, the Lotus 97T and

ABOVE The instrument panel mounting acted as a forward roll hoop, which, combined with the rear roll-over bar, formed a driver safety cell. The right-hand gearshift controls a traditional H-pattern gate. The carbonfibre seat was moulded to exactly match the driver's shape. *(James Ward)*

BELOW The Momo steering wheel rim is made of Alcantara, a man-made suede material. *(James Ward)*

98T have a three-pedal configuration, with a conventional clutch.

On the lower right-hand side of the cockpit, the carbonfibre-topped gear lever has a traditional H-gate configuration for the five or six speeds and is linked to the transmission by a steel rod. Just ahead of the gear lever is a mushroom-shaped 'pull' button for the onboard fire extinguishers. On the driver's left is a brake distribution lever that allows the bias of front-to-rear braking to be adjusted.

Ahead of the driver, the Momo steering wheel utilises a padded rim made of Alcantara, which is a man-made suede offering a soft surface and non-slip grip. In contrast to modern cars, the steering wheel carries just two small push buttons, mounted on its aluminium centre. A green button on the right operates the radio and a red button on the left activates a 'push-to-pass' function, which overrides the turbocharger wastegate controls for a short period to allow extra horsepower for overtaking. As a precaution in the event of a failure in the wiring from the steering wheel, these two buttons are repeated on the lower part of the instrument panel.

Two large analogue dials made by French instrument maker Brion-Leroux dominate the instrument panel. With yellow symbols on black faces, they indicate engine revs and turbocharger boost. Below the panel, toggle switches control ignition, low-visibility rear 'fog' light, pitlane speed limiter and radio master switch. There are rotary controls on the lower right of the panel for ride-height adjustment and a five-position turbocharger boost control.

In race conditions, the boost control was a critical item as it controlled fuel consumption. As a result of Senna running out of fuel in several races in 1985, an 'annunciator' panel was added to the 98T above the main dashboard to supply additional information, provided by a fuel-management computer that calculated consumption based on fuel flow, boost and throttle setting. This information allowed the driver to adapt his driving style or tactics to ensure that he could finish the race on the 195-litre allocation.

In the 97T two small LCD (liquid crystal display) screens gave the driver digital information on coolant and temperature levels. This was developed with the 98T in the form of a single digital display across the top of the panel inside the windscreen giving, from left, read-outs of the critical factors of turbocharger temperature (typically 1,120 degrees centigrade), induction air and coolant temperature (80 and 90 degrees centigrade respectively), fuel consumption and exhaust temperature.

The digital display is surmounted with three warning lights. Positioned in the driver's immediate line of vision, these indicate red for low oil pressure, blue for alternator charge and green to remind the driver when the car is in neutral.

Suspension and steering

The wheelbase of the Lotus 97T and 98T is similar to their predecessors at 2,720mm, slightly shorter than their McLaren and Williams rivals, but a little longer than the similarly powered Renault RE50's 2,600mm, although this was subsequently increased to 2,800mm on the later RE60 to accommodate the slightly longer Renault RE15 engine package. In the case of the two Lotus chassis, Ducarouge, by virtue of clever packaging, was able to maintain the same wheelbase for successive seasons.

Both Team Lotus cars also share a similar 1,816mm front track and 1,620mm rear, both measurements at the limit of the dimensions specified by FISA. The widest possible front track was deemed necessary both in terms of chassis stability and to smooth airflow to the radiators and around the sidepods, while the rear track likewise was as wide as possible to allow maximum width for the low-level rear aerodynamic diffuser and to minimise aerodynamic interference from airflow over the rear tyres. When combined with 11in wide front tyres and 16in rears, the car was within millimetres of the mandated maximum width of 2,150mm.

Steel suspension arms and pull-rods are attached to magnesium suspension uprights incorporating steel axles and large-diameter, low-friction wheel bearings. Attention to fine detail even runs to tiny bleed tubes in the uprights, designed to allow the venting of moisture trapped during the cars' transport between factory and track. For a brief period following the 1986 San Marino Grand Prix, where the Lotus 97T cars retired with driveshaft failures attributed to excess flexing of the rear uprights, the cars reverted to 1985 rear suspension components. However, by the Canadian Grand Prix, Senna's car had moved back to the lighter 1986 specification, which also allowed hydraulic ride-height control dampers to be used. Dumfries's car was updated in time for the mid-season French Grand Prix.

Ducarouge introduced a further refinement to the manufacture of the steel suspension components. They were made from 15CDV6 steel, which had been developed for the aerospace industry in France and can be recognised by its distinctive mottled appearance. Unlike the more commonly used SAE 4130 specification, the specialist French steel does not require heat treatment to harden the material, and the absence of chromium and molybdenum hardening mediums also means that it is easier to weld and fabricate.

At the inboard end of the suspension, within the chassis, Koni oil-filled dampers and integral titanium or steel coil springs provide the suspension medium. The rocker and pull-rod suspension units had developed since the 1970s to allow the main suspension units to be carried within the chassis, aiding aerodynamic performance, minimising unsprung weight and optimising load paths.

The minimisation of unsprung weight was, and remains, a key area of suspension design. Comprising components such as axles, wheel bearings, hubs, outboard brakes, wheels, tyres

and a portion of the weight of driveshafts and suspension links, unsprung weight adds to suspension inertia, reducing the ability of the wheels and tyres to react to bumps, reducing grip. While the high temperature generated by brake components on the Lotus 97T and 98T required that they remain 'outboard' for better cooling, moving the key suspension spring and damper units 'inboard' represented a significant contribution to the reduction of unsprung weight.

While the 97T's suspension utilises pull-rod front links to the inboard spring/damper units and rocker-type rear links, the later 98T has pull-rod units at the rear too. Rocker-arm units have to operate in both tension and compression, so they have to be of more robust

Maintaining a minimum ride height was critical to cornering performance during the 1980s because control of the airflow under the car contributed significantly to the creation of under-car venturi effects, which generated aerodynamic downforce and hence grip. This first resulted in a trend to ever-stiffer suspension, with high spring rates and minimum travel, reaching its peak early in the decade with the skirted 'ground-effect' cars that were sometimes described as '1,000 horsepower go-karts'.

From the 1983 season the advent of the 'flat-bottom' regulations put an end to under-car venturi tunnels in an attempt to reduce cornering speeds, and a minimum 6cm gap was required between the track and the car's floor. Team Lotus engineers discovered that the level of under-car aerodynamic downforce was highly sensitive to any change in ride height, such as when the car rose on its suspension as the fuel load reduced, and so for the 1985 and 1986 seasons the Lotus 97T and 98T featured an innovation in the form of hydraulic ride-height control, utilising the car's suspension dampers.

Lotus Cars, in fact, had developed 'active ride' on the road-going Lotus Esprit sports car. As early as 1983 Team Lotus had raced fully reactive hydraulic suspension on the Cosworth-powered Lotus 92, achieving sixth place in that year's Detroit Grand Prix. However, that system, using a hydraulic pump to pressurise computer-controlled hydro-pneumatic suspension units, had various disadvantages:

processing the volume of data generated from electronic load sensors around the car proved to be challenging; engine power was sapped as the hydraulic pump cost around 10bhp; and the components, associated pipework and wiring added more than 20kg to the car's weight.

The ride-height system for the 97T and 98T was simpler, more compact and lighter. It simply linked a switch on the car's dashboard to a small hydraulic valve on a small pressure chamber on top of each damper. As the fuel load reduced, the driver pulled on the cockpit control, opening the valve, whereupon the car's weight would vent the hydraulic fluid. This reduced the 'pre-load' pressure in the damper, allowing the ride height to settle to the stipulated minimum.

The system, of course, was irreversible, so if the driver triggered it too early he would have to cope with the car potentially bottoming on the track. A signal was therefore arranged, with yellow downward-facing arrows shown on the driver's pit board to remind him of the right moment to trigger the system.

Ride-height control was subsequently further refined in the 98T to become a two-stage system, allowing the height to be optimised twice in each race.

The system was deemed to be an important factor in maximising the aerodynamic downforce of the 98T, and was also an important 'halfway house' to the introduction of fully active, computer-controlled suspension on the subsequent Lotus-Honda 99T for the 1987 season.

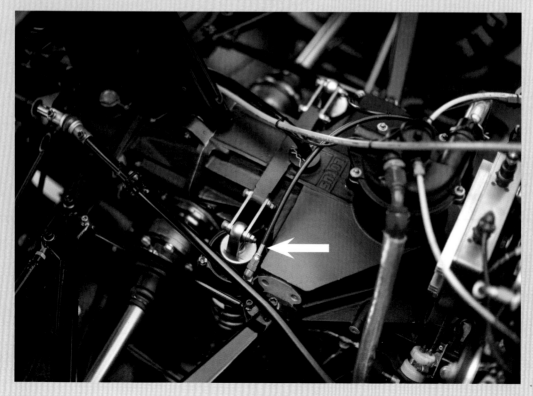

LEFT The innovative ride-height control was activated from the cockpit, releasing pneumatic pre-load on the dampers. *(James Ward)*

construction to resist flexing, creating a weight penalty. The move to pull-rods, which operate in tension only, allowed the links to be lighter.

While suspension spring rates were high, to maintain minimum ride height and aid under-car aerodynamics, there was still fine-tuning capability, with each corner of the car being individually adjustable in castor, camber and ride height. In addition, changes to spring rates would be used to soften the suspension, aiding turn-in and traction on slower tracks such as Monaco or Detroit, where mechanical grip was more important than raw aerodynamic downforce.

The non-assisted steering used a rack-and-pinion system that was essentially identical to that used by rivals including Brabham, McLaren, Tyrrell and Williams. A bought-in item, it was produced by Jack Knight Developments, who had originally started in motorsport as the manufacturer of straight-cut gearboxes for competition Mini Coopers.

Wheels and tyres

As with all Formula 1 cars of the era, the Lotus 97T and 98T used magnesium alloy wheels of 13in diameter, with widths of 11.5in at the front and 16.25in at the rear.

Initially the cars raced on split-rim wheels, built by Speedline in Italy, with inner and outer spun-aluminium rims secured by 16 bolts

to an eight-spoke inner section in sand-cast magnesium. The split-rim Speedline wheels were replaced during the 1986 season by British-made Dymag wheels produced as single magnesium castings, which brought a total saving of 2.0–2.5kg in unsprung weight.

The wheels and tyres are fitted to a bell-shaped alloy wheel carrier attached to the axle, braking unit and wheel bearing, with acceleration and braking loads carried by eight drive pegs on each hub. A single, specially shaped, spin-on wheel nut on a threaded central spigot with a spring-loaded safety pin enables quick removal and replacement during pit-stops.

Goodyear Eagle F1 radial-ply racing tyres had been used by Team Lotus since the start of the 1984 season and the tyres were effectively the 'standard fit' among the leading teams; McLaren, Williams and Ferrari were similarly shod, only Brabham, Benetton and Ligier opting for the alternative Pirelli tyres. Goodyear's racing operation would fit and pressurise tyres in its own dedicated paddock facility for collection by a team's mechanics.

Goodyear had introduced radial-ply tyre construction for its slick racing tyres from the start of 1983. Their stiffer construction, compared with previous bias-belted 'crossply' tyres, allowed the tread to form a more constant contact patch, but the tyres typically operated their best at smaller slip angles, demanding more precise driving. The 1984 Monaco Grand Prix saw Goodyear introduce its first wet-weather racing radial to Formula 1 and this featured for the first time the unidirectional 'gatorback' tread pattern to improve wet-weather traction.

For the Lotus 97T and 98T, five different compounds of slick tyre were available, graded A to E from softest to hardest. Owing to their high grip and short life, the softest A-compound tyres were used principally in qualifying on tracks such as Hockenheim or Montréal, where cornering loads were low. The usual race compounds – B, C or D – were selected based on track wear characteristics

and ambient temperature, while the hardest E-compound tyres were used only on tracks such as the then new Hungaroring and Jerez circuits, which involved high-downforce settings, frequent braking, tight corners, high ambient temperatures and an abrasive, dusty surface.

Tyre-tread temperatures, generated by friction between tyre and track, were a critical factor influenced by driving style, suspension set-up, fuel load, ambient temperature and tyre pressures. A typical slick racing tyre operates best with a tread temperature of around 100 degrees centigrade, about the same as a boiling kettle. If the temperature is too low, grip deteriorates, creating added wear as the tread slides on the track surface. Conversely, if the tread becomes too hot, over 130 degrees, grip is lost as the rubber compounds in the tread

HEATED TYRES

A new addition to the Team Lotus pit garage during the 1986 season was the introduction of electrically heated tyre warmers. Teams had been aware for some years of the advantage of pre-warming tyres by wrapping them in blankets or covers, and some had even put tyres in black plastic dustbin liners and left them in the sun. However Mike Drury, a Formula 1 fan and the head of Dorset-based clothing manufacturer MA Horne, had a novel idea.

'I saw that the teams were trying to keep the cars' tyres warm by wrapping them in blankets and duvets,' said Mike. 'It occurred to me, since I was already in the business of making weatherproof jackets and anoraks, that here was an opportunity.' Drury came up with the idea of a bespoke electrically heated blanket that kept the tyres at between 80 to 100 degrees until just a few seconds before they were fitted to a car.

Ironically Team Lotus's great rival, Williams, was the first to demonstrate the advantage of Drury's concept. In the closing stages of the 1986 Spanish Grand Prix at Jerez, Nigel Mansell used pre-warmed tyres in a pit-stop only a few laps from the end of the race. With them, Mansell charged though the field from fifth place to second, only losing to Ayrton Senna's Lotus by 0.014sec. Needless to say, Team Lotus was Drury's next customer!

Brakes

The internal diameter of the wheels effectively governed the size of the car's brakes, with both discs and calipers required to fit inside the wheel rims. Team Lotus utilised braking systems provided by Italian manufacturer Brembo, which included 11in diameter discs with pads activated by a single four-piston caliper on each wheel. The team had previously toyed with dual calipers but their additional unsprung weight and complexity meant that the single-caliper design was retained.

Brembo's aluminium calipers and pistons were regarded as the most efficient means available of transmitting a driver's braking effort from the hydraulic system to the brake pads. In earlier seasons Team Lotus had combined them with Ferodo asbestos-based friction materials and inch-thick cast-iron brake discs. From 1985, however, the Lotus 97T and 98T introduced to the team a new technology – carbon-on-carbon braking.

Carbon brakes

Carbon braking technology had its roots in the Anglo-French collaboration on Concorde, which had demanded a wholly new braking solution to handle its combination of weight and high landing speed. French aerospace company SEP, later to become Carbon Industrie, was at the forefront of the developments and was therefore the ideal partner for Team Lotus.

The new discs and pads utilised a high-density mix of carbon and rayon fibres which

ABOVE With no refuelling, pit-stops for tyre changes were a race-winning factor. *(John Townsend, F1 Pictures)*

degrade, and there is a risk of the tread material blistering or even failing completely.

While changes from one tyre compound to another could be made during a race, such as choosing to use a softer compound for early-race pace, it was not, unlike today, obligatory to change tyre types. Indeed, as drivers sometimes drove with minimum boost later in the race to conserve fuel, a set of softer-compound tyres might be used later in the race merely to maintain tyre-tread temperature.

BELOW The internal diameter of the wheels effectively governed the size of the car's brake discs. *(John Townsend, F1 Pictures)*

BELOW RIGHT The 11in-diameter brake discs were made from a high-density mix of carbon and rayon fibres, and each disc carries a single Brembo four-piston caliper. *(Author)*

were repeatedly cured in a high-temperature oven where additional carbon particles were added. The process, known as 'carbon vapour processing', or more often 'densification', resulted in a material of such phenomenal hardness that it could only be machined using diamond tooling, but offered a significantly higher coefficient of friction for increased braking effort and could ultimately withstand temperatures of up to 900 degrees centigrade. A further benefit was lighter weight, reducing both unsprung and overall weight as well as offering lower rotating inertia, further aiding potential deceleration.

As with the earlier cast-iron discs, the new SEP carbon units featured internal radial slots to ventilate them with cooler air, distributed by internal vanes. However, temperature control at both ends of the spectrum was critical. While overheating and degradation, causing loss of efficiency and premature wear, was one factor, insufficient heat would cause the brakes to suffer 'glazing' due to chemical reactions of the bonding materials on their contact surfaces.

Once the brakes were glazed, the car would suffer significantly poorer retardation and in most cases the situation could not be remedied, no matter how hard the brakes were subsequently applied. To avoid this, therefore, the car had to be driven aggressively from the moment of leaving the pitlane. Clearly this was not a problem with drivers such as Ayrton Senna in the team!

Engine

Developed in natural evolution from the EF3, Renault's first aluminium-block V6 Formula 1 engine, the Renault EF4 engine used by Team Lotus during 1985 and the EF15 used during both the 1985 and 1986 seasons were the ultimate expressions of the 1980s turbo era. Light in weight and potent, they were much more driveable than the early turbos (with 'light-switch' power delivery), and many of their technical features – including electronic engine management, multi-point and common-rail fuel injection systems, and coil-on-plug ignition – would find their way on to subsequent road cars.

Renault's investment in its Formula 1 programme was substantial. It was reported

that during 1985 alone the company spent around US $27 million on engine development and its Formula 1 engine department, under the management of Bernard Dudot, employed 85 staff and annually produced 40 engines, of which 15 were prepared for the 'works' team, the remaining 'customer' engines being prepared by sub-contractors. In 1984 and 1985 Team Lotus's engines were prepared by Mecachrome at Bourges, while in 1986, with Lotus now having 'works team' status, the engines were delivered direct from Renault Sport's Viry-Châtillon headquarters. It is to the credit of both operations that there was little perceived difference in quality between the two suppliers.

The Renault EF4 engine's dimensions are 640mm high (to the top of the induction plenum chambers), 640mm wide (between the cam covers) and 480mm long. Including turbo system, clutch and starter, the engine weighs 160kg and revs to a maximum of 10,500rpm.

During 1984, the Renault engineers began work on a fundamental update of the engine, which had until then continued to follow the architecture of the original Renault turbo engine of the 1970s. The result was the EF15 with a longer-stroke, smaller-bore cylinder block, which allowed better internal cooling via larger waterways, while the smaller piston crowns also aided better heat dissipation. A total of around 50 EF15 engines were built.

Despite its longer stroke, the EF15 could be revved to 12,000rpm from the outset. It weighs 154kg, including turbo system, clutch and starter. It is 20mm lower, aiding 'packaging'

Rightly described as the father of the turbocharged Formula 1 engine, Bernard Dudot first became involved with its development in 1973, having been appointed by Jean Rédéle, founder of sports car maker and tuner Alpine, to lead the dedicated competition engine department started by the company in 1967. After Alpine was merged with Gordini in 1973 to create Renault Sport, Dudot began working alongside fellow engineers François Castaing and Jean-Pierre Boudy to adapt the existing normally aspirated 2-litre V6 sports car engine to turbocharged configuration.

Management reorganisations in early 1975 saw Castaing take on a greater administrative role and eventually move to road-car engineering, while Boudy was placed in charge of the design office. This left Dudot in charge of a programme to develop a sports car engine for

RIGHT Bernard Dudot – architect of Renault turbo power. *(Renault Sport)*

BELOW Ayrton Senna and Bernard Dudot (right) discuss engine performance. *(John Townsend, F1 Pictures)*

Le Mans and a secret 1.5-litre turbo for Formula 1. That engine, the Renault-Gordini EF1, made its début in the Renault Sport RS01 at the 1977 British Grand Prix at Silverstone.

By the time Team Lotus and Renault cemented their relationship in 1983, turbocharged Renault EF1 and EF3 engines had already won 11 grands prix for Jean-Pierre Jabouille, René Arnoux and Alain Prost. The 1983 season saw Prost score five more victories in the turbo-powered Renault Sport RS05, only narrowly losing out to Nelson Piquet in the Drivers' Championship.

The 1984 season was fallow in comparison. Prost, damagingly critical of the Renault Sport team, had moved to the dominant McLaren operation, leaving the French team mired in politics. Dudot, though, continued to work behind the scenes developing both the EF4*bis* and longer-stroke EF15 units for Renault Sport as well as for customer teams Ligier and Team Lotus. His dogged persistance was to pay off with victories for Ayrton Senna and Elio de Angelis in the Lotus-Renault 97T at the 1985 Portuguese, San Marino and Belgian Grands Prix. In 1986 he devised the revolutionary EF14B unit, featuring *Distribution Pneumatique* pneumatic valve operation.

In 1987, after Renault's temporary withdrawal from Formula 1, Dudot began work on an equally revolutionary engine. His 3.5-litre V10 engine combined the compactness of a V8 with the torque of a V12 and became the dominant force in Formula 1 upon Renault's return. In 1992, with Nigel Mansell's Williams-Renault FW14B, Dudot finally achieved his ambition of powering a Formula 1 World Champion.

Bernard Dudot was described by Francophile British Formula 1 journalist Joe Saward as a man with 'the eyes of a lost and hungry dog, but there lurks a little twinkle of mischief. He speaks English with an accent which would have won him film parts in Hollywood in the 1930s. His passion is engines and, on his occasional weekend off, he can be found at French provincial race tracks, his sleeves rolled up and hands greasy, working on *Formule Renault* engines.'

Still active at tracks in his mid-70s, Dudot, with that twinkle in his eye, would be the first to appreciate the compliment.

and aerodynamic performance, and 40mm narrower at the top, owing to the inlet trumpets being angled inwards to create lower-set and more closely spaced plenum chambers. The EF15 is slightly longer than its predecessor due to a 50mm extension to the clutch bellhousing to accommodate a sensor for the electronic engine control unit.

In addition to the new EF15 engine, for the 1985 season an EF4*bis* power unit was developed from the existing EF4 short-stroke engine, its specification partly derived from EF15 developments and featuring around 30% new parts, including a revised turbo installation. The EF4*bis* was available in low-compression (7:1), high-boost form for qualifying, where it developed over 1,000bhp at 4.5 bar boost, or in race specification with higher compression (7.5:1) and lower boost, although this was to prove less fuel efficient than the longer-stroke EF15.

Due to supply difficulties with the short-stroke EF4 unit during 1985, EF4*bis* and EF15 engines were both used in the Lotus 97T, emphasis switching to the new EF15 engine once it became fully available. The Lotus 98T for the 1986 season was designed to utilise only the EF15 unit and its variants.

Supply chains were necessarily convoluted between Renault Sport and Team Lotus. During the European racing season a van would be driven from Norfolk to Paris ahead of each race to collect the qualifying engines for installation at Ketteringham Hall, with Renault Sport trucks then bringing the race engines direct to the track.

The final derivatives of the EF15, known as the EF15*bis* and EF15C, were developed during the 1986 season and featured a new electronic ignition system, redesigned cylinder heads and *Distribution Pneumatique* valve actuation. The EF15C additionally featured further cylinder-head changes for improved water circulation, reprofiled inlet tracts, and modified exhaust and fuel injection systems. It is said that in 1986

ABOVE The Renault EF15 installation on the Lotus 98T was the most sophisticated of the time. *(John Townsend, F1 Pictures)*

BELOW The EF15 unit featured a longer stroke and smaller cylinder bore than its predecessors, for greater race fuel efficiency. *(Author)*

Team Lotus spent more than 40% of its budget on the upgraded EF15 engines.

In addition to these fundamental changes, the engine specification continually evolved as engineers sought to exploit every technical advantage. These updates were designated alphabetically, and by the end of the 1986 season the ultimate 'G' specification of the EF15C used by Ayrton Senna in unlimited-boost qualifying form at the Australian Grand Prix in Adelaide was capable of being briefly 'over-revved' up to 13,500rpm and was estimated to produce over 1,300bhp.

No one knows with certainty just how high the final rated horsepower really was. The Renault Sport dynamometers at Viry-Châtillon were calibrated to a maximum of around 1,100bhp, and it is said that in the final tests of the EF15C that figure was passed with several hundred rpm still to go and with the read-outs going off the top of the chart!

Cylinder block

The Renault EF4 cylinder block, the first to be cast in-house by Renault, maintained the asymmetric V6 configuration and dimensions of both the earlier EF3 aluminium blocks cast by sub-contractor Messier and the original cast-iron blocks of the original Renault turbo engines of the late 1970s.

While maintaining the bore and stroke of 86mm x 42.6mm, giving a capacity of 1,492cc, the EF4 engine has thicker walls to give the cylinder block greater rigidity. This allows it to handle higher compression ratios, boost and engine torque, and also reduces potential flexing in its role as a stressed component in a car's chassis.

Incorporating the cylinder barrels, water and oil pathways and the upper crankcase, the aluminium block was cast as a single unit and finished by CNC (Computer Numerical Control). A separate alloy lower crankcase carries the four plain main bearings, with supplementary elements providing additional reinforcement for the main-bearing mountings. Eight long studs extending from the bottom facing edge of the cylinder block secure the lower crankcase, while a further eight long carry-through studs on each side of the main cylinder-block vee secure each cylinder head.

The EF15 cylinder block is cast on similar lines to its predecessor, but with cylinder bores reduced from 86mm to 80.1mm. The required capacity of 1,492cc was regained by the use of a longer-throw 49.4mm crankshaft.

A flat flange at the rear of the cylinder block makes up the mounting point for the clutch and gearbox housing, attached to the engine by six 14mm studs. At the lower front edge of the block, a separate aluminium casting acts as the lower mounting point to the back of the monocoque, while the upper mountings are attached to the forward ends of the cylinder heads.

OPPOSITE The EF15C version was the ultimate evolution of the Renault V6 turbo's decade-long development. *(James Ward)*

BELOW The entire engine, including turbochargers and intercoolers, can be rapidly removed as a single unit. *(Author)*

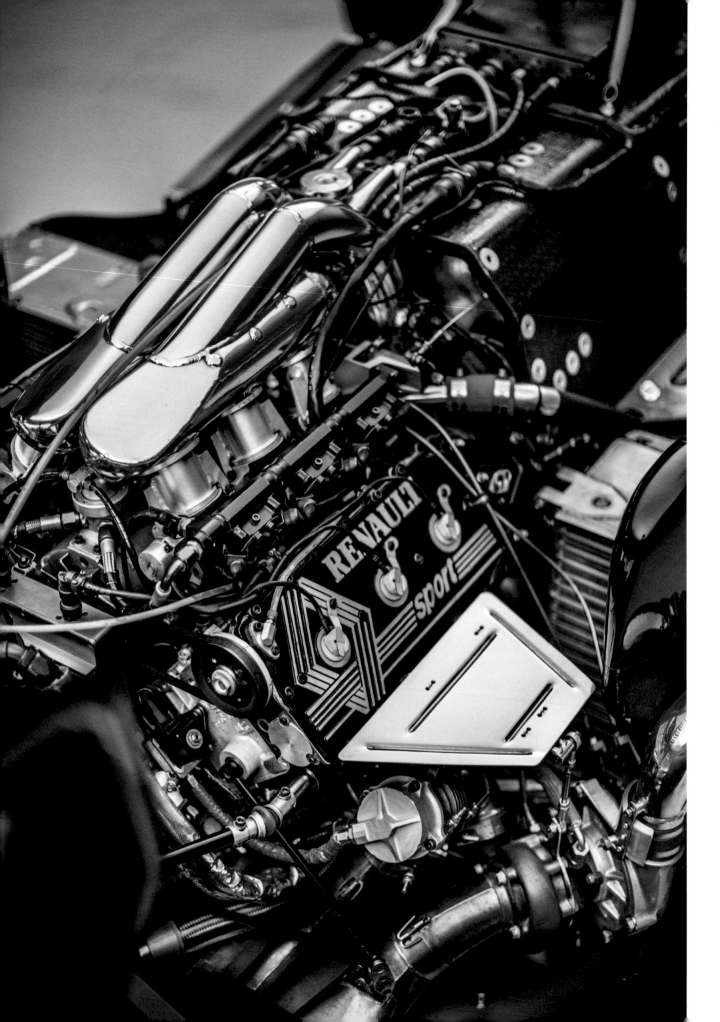

The EF4 and EF15 engines were designed to be quickly removable from the car and replaced. If required, the entire power unit – including the engine, turbochargers, wastegates, intercoolers and exhausts – can be removed from the car as a single integrated item.

Both the EF4 and EF15 engines feature combined electronic fuel injection and ignition systems controlled by a central electronic control unit (ECU). The firing order for both engines is 1–6–3–5–2–4. The evolution of digital electronic systems and both common-rail and multi-point fuel injection systems were developed through the engines' lives.

Cylinder liners

Both the EF4 and EF15 engines utilise Nikasil 'wet' aluminium liners, inserted into the cylinder block for maximum heat dissipation and water circulation. The liners are only located at the top end of the cylinders, leaving them free to expand at their lower ends. Sealing is provided by Viton 'O' ring seals.

Replacement of the liners allowed the cylinder blocks to be reused after routine overhaul and crack testing, based on 'lifed' usage. Should an engine failure have damaged the block beyond the liners, however, the normal procedure was to scrap the block, melting down and reusing the alloy in other castings.

Crankshaft and connecting rods

Running in four plain Glyco main bearings, the three-pin crankshaft is machined from solid steel then nitrided, and features extended balance webs on the crank flanges. No vibration damper was found to be required, so the nose of the crankshaft merely contains the camshaft drive, while a flange at the rear of the crankshaft provides the attachment for the flywheel, secured with 12 13mm bolts.

The camshaft drive is taken from the front of the crank, with a gear on the nose driving a gear on each side of the engine, transmitting power via external toothed belts to each cylinder bank. In addition to the double overhead camshafts, associated pulleys also drive oil and water pumps mounted low down on each side of the crankcase, and the alternator drive is taken from the left-side inlet camshaft. The main fuel pump drive is also taken from the front of the crankshaft.

Short nitride-steel connecting rods have plain Glyco big-end bearings, each secured at the bottom end by two high-tensile steel bolts. The little-end bearings are secured via free-floating gudgeon pins in each piston.

Pistons

The six Mahle aluminium pistons, 86mm diameter in the EF4 and 80.6mm in the EF15, each feature three Goetze piston rings and have flat tops, pocketed to allow valve clearance. The design of both the pistons and the combustion chambers were the subject of continuing development and evolution through the life of the engines in the search for both maximum power and the most efficient lean-burn processes to meet the requirements of the 220-litre and 195-litre 'fuel economy' regulations.

Lower compression with higher turbocharger pressure was the norm for qualifying, while higher compressions, allied to lower turbo boost, allowed a better blend of performance and fuel economy in a race. The higher compression ratios were attained by developing taller pistons that intruded higher into the combustion chambers.

The pistons also feature oil gallery circulation, with jets spraying oil on to the underside of the pistons to reduce piston-crown temperatures, a design element initially borrowed from heavy diesel engines. Oil is introduced to a circular oil channel within the piston through an access aperture and is distributed by the reciprocating movement of the piston in a 'cocktail-shaker effect' before draining though a second aperture under the crown.

As the maximum thermal loading of an engine is limited by what pistons, rings, valves and valve seats can withstand, Renault, Mahle and Goetze engineers worked together to develop materials to operate in the highest possible temperatures. This included experimental work on high-temperature alloys, steels and ceramics for pistons and rings.

Cylinder heads

The two aluminium-alloy cylinder heads, one for each block, each carry separate cam covers with the camshaft bearing caps formed by the cam cover. The heads feature a single spark

ABOVE A flat flange at the rear of the engine forms the mounting point for the clutch and gearbox. *(James Ward)*

sodium-filled valves are set at 10 degrees from the cylinder axis and the exhaust valves at 11.5 degrees, creating an included valve angle of 21.5 degrees. The valve-head diameters remained unchanged on both the Renault EF4 and EF15 engines at 29.8mm for the inlet valve and 26.1mm for the exhaust valve.

The cylinder block-to-head sealing on both engines is by use of a composite metallic gasket for gas sealing with Viton ring seals for the oil and water passages. A notable issue during high-boost qualifying running was extreme heat soak annealing the cylinder heads, causing the aluminium to soften and distort, leading to compression loss and fluid leaks.

The EF4 and early EF15 engines featured valves that were activated by steel bucket tappets housed in the cam carrier and closed by coaxial valve springs produced by Schmittheim. These springs were highly stressed due to the steep cam profiles required to achieve the required valve opening, and in the ultimate Renault EF15*bis* and EF15C engines they were replaced by the *Distribution Pneumatique* pneumatic valve-control system.

On the EF15 engine the upper monocoque

plug and four valves per cylinder, driven by twin overhead belt-driven camshafts per head, giving the engine a 4-OHC configuration. Each nitrided steel camshaft runs in four plain Glyco bearings.

Each cylinder head contains three combustion chambers that are optimised for thermodynamic efficiency, both in handling combustion temperatures and maximising heat transfer to the car's cooling system by waterways surrounding the chambers. The

DISTRIBUTION PNEUMATIQUE

An innovative new valve control system was a feature of the EF15*bis* engine during the 1986 season. *Distribution Pneumatique* (DP) provided a valve-closing system, replacing mechanical springs on the inlet and exhaust valves. Conventional valve springs were reaching their limits in closing the valves sufficiently quickly at high revs and handling the aggressive camshaft profiles in use, while their high spring-compression rating was also causing fatigue failures.

Renault engineers explored the use of mechanical desmodromic control, with the valves closed by a cam-and-leverage system, but rejected this as too heavy and complex. Instead they devised a system using compressed nitrogen gas at 1.2–1.8 bar as the pressure medium to close the valves. The gas is stored in a pressure chamber in the space normally occupied by the springs, with an additional 0.5-litre nitrogen bottle in the vee between the cylinders acting as a reserve, a pressure-control valve allowing the six individual pressure chambers to be automatically replenished if required. A flange on the stem of each valve acts in effect as a piston, with the

nitrogen gas pressure acting as the medium to force the valves to comply with the cam profile more consistently.

In addition to providing greater mechanical efficiency and reducing the risk of 'valve float', the system was found to create a self-damping effect that reduced potential vibration. Unlike mechanical valve springs, which can suffer stress or fatigue failure if the engine is over-revved, the DP system is much more tolerant of higher engine speeds.

It was found that by increasing the nitrogen pressure, the effect was equivalent to fitting stiffer valve springs, enabling higher maximum revs, with 13,000rpm being attained during the 1986 season. In addition, the ability to briefly 'over-rev' the engine with a lower risk of damage allowed drivers to be more aggressive on downshifting, to aid braking into slower corners and to hold a gear at maximum revs on a long corner, avoiding the destabilising change in load with a gearshift. A final benefit was lower weight, with around 2.5kg being saved. As this weight loss was at the top end of the engine, the engine's centre of gravity was also lowered.

LEFT The front of the engine accommodates the belt drives for the oil and water pumps and twin overhead camshafts on each cylinder head. *(Author)*

mounting points form part of the cam covers, with the higher location point optimising the load paths of the stressed engine/chassis structure. The earlier EF4 engines take the mounting points from the block/head interface.

Turbochargers

The heart of the Renault engine's phenomenal power-to-capacity ratio is its pair of Garrett turbochargers. Renault Sport had initially used German KKK turbochargers on earlier EF4 engines, but had switched to the American manufacturer by the time of the advent of the Lotus 97T and 98T, with custom-made turbos combining Garrett T-04 and T-05 production components with specially designed input turbine and compressor vane combinations.

Based on maintaining the typical optimum air-to-fuel mixture of approximately 10:1, by compressing and thus multiplying the effective volume of air entering the engine, in theory a similar additional proportion of fuel can be burned at any one time. This allows a turbocharged engine to deliver a proportionate increase in power. In practice around 75% efficiency was the best that could be achieved.

Mounted behind the radiators and intercooler at the rear of the sidepods, the turbochargers each contain an exhaust-driven, single-stage, radial-flow turbine located on one side in a distinctive spiral-shaped, cast-iron housing. The turbine is fed from the triple-branch exhaust manifold from each bank of cylinders. Heated by the exhaust gases spinning the inlet turbine, the exhaust-fed turbine operates at

over 90,000rpm and a typical temperature of between 1,100–1,150 degrees centigrade.

The exceedingly high temperatures require the use of silicon 'firesleeve' or 'refrasil' calcium silicate thermal insulation on oil pipes and sensor cables as well as heat shields beneath the bodywork in the vicinity of the turbocharger and exhaust system. The heat also necessitates the use of high-temperature steel for the cast turbocharger impeller, which is welded

LEFT Garrett AiResearch turbochargers were responsible for the engine's huge horsepower. *(Author)*

LEFT A wastegate for each turbocharger controlled pressure from the engine exhaust system. *(Author)*

ABOVE **After being compressed by the turbocharger, the inlet air is passed through large air-to-air intercoolers in order to reduce temperature and increase density.** *(Author)*

on to the rotor shaft that in turn runs via an internal bearing, pressure-fed with oil from the engine, to the 'cool' compressor side of the turbocharger assembly.

The compressor unit is housed in a larger-diameter aluminium casing that contains a cast-aluminium-alloy compressor turbine clamped to the end of the shaft by a locking nut. This pressurises inlet air drawn in via ducts in the top of the sidepod, before the compressed air is then cooled by large 'intercoolers' prior to being introduced to the engine via twin plenum chambers on top of the inlet tracts.

The exhaust gases, meanwhile, leave the inlet turbine via a single manifold with a dual-split exit on each side of the car. In addition, a single third pipe on each side ejects blow-by exhaust gases from the boost-controlling wastegate. All six exhausts then blow on to the carbonfibre rear aerodynamic diffuser, enhancing downforce.

RIGHT **The heat generated by excessive boost could even melt the turbochargers.** *(Classic Team Lotus)*

Intercoolers

The role of the intercoolers is to remove heat, which is generated by compression of the inlet air and the high ambient temperature surrounding it in the turbo. This heat would otherwise adversely affect the air density, which limits the amount of fuel that can be burned in an optimum mixture.

The twin SECAN air-to-air intercoolers, prominently mounted in the sidepods behind the radiators and ahead of the turbochargers, duct ambient air through 20 horizontal elements, reducing the temperature of the outlet air from the turbocharger from 240 degrees to around 40 degrees before it enters the induction system.

Typically a 10-degree increase in charge temperature can reduce power output by 25bhp, but sometimes the consequences can be more severe. Early in the development of the EF4 engine, excessive charge temperatures caused the fuel/air mixture to become sufficiently rich for the lubricating oil to be washed off the cylinder barrels, leading to catastrophic engine failures.

The pressurised air from each turbocharger is fed via an aluminium duct to the outside rear of the intercooler, being transmitted via its own pressure through micro-bore pipes across the cooler deck. The cooled air is then forced from the inside of the cooler via a long, prominent aluminium duct into the plenum chamber, which is designed to allow a more balanced distribution of the charge air prior to being combined with fuel in the car's induction system.

TURBO LAG

One of the prime requirements of turbocharger design, in addition to optimising its ultimate 'adibatic' or pumping efficiency, is to ensure that it offers the most efficient profile of boost across the wide range of turbine speeds created by the different engine revs and loads experienced by a racing engine. Careful attention to detail in areas such as the size of the turbine entry nozzle and exhaust dimensions, as well as the optimising of a carefully matched relationship between engine revs, throttle setting and ignition timing, form a key part of fine tuning the engine's responsiveness.

The mechanical inertia of the turbine 'spooling up' from low revs creates the phenomenon known as 'turbo lag', which leads to a delay between pressing the throttle and power being delivered. In the early days of turbocharger development, this delay and the subsequent surge of power was described by Renault Sport test driver Jean-Pierre Jabouille as being akin to the level of control one has when pressing the button on an elevator. The Renault EF4 and EF15 power units for the Lotus 97T and 98T therefore utilised cutting-edge developments to reduce this effect to a minimum.

Renault chief engineer Bernard Dudot once described the secret behind developing greater driveability as designing the entire engine and turbocharger as a single integrated component. Improvements to electronic engine management and fuel-injection systems made significant contributions to driveability, while the dimensions of both inlet pipework and primary exhaust pipework were kept as short as possible to prevent lag, with the EF15 engine having its turbochargers moved as close as possible to the cylinder block to achieve this. The turbo impeller and compressor discs and blades are also finely tuned for weight and optimised in terms of aerodynamic efficiency.

In 1984 Renault engineer Jean-Pierre Boudy patented DPV, which stands for *Dispositif Pre-rotation Variable* (variable pre-rotation device), as a means of 'ensuring near-instantaneous throttle response from a competition turbocharged engine'. This system, located in a distinctive disc-shaped housing ahead of the compressor, is essentially a multi-variable nozzle arrangement, mechanically linked to the throttle. According to throttle position, it controls the direction and area of air that hits the compressor wheel, ensuring that the turbine idles at a higher speed than it would with a fixed intake. The higher the compressor idle speed, the shorter the time it will take to reach its operating speed, resulting in less lag.

Other innovations included the fitment ahead of the compressor of guide vanes that stall the airflow at low power settings, further reducing drag and allowing the turbo to keep spinning. In addition, the throttle butterflies in the two inlet manifolds are also tuned to enhance turbo response. When the throttle is closed, a carefully calculated amount of blow-by is allowed to leak past the control. This in turn prevents over-pressurisation of the manifold and undue drag on the turbocharger outlet vanes.

BELOW Special turbocharger inlet systems were patented by Renault to minimise turbo lag by stalling the compressor blades to reduce off-throttle drag. *(Renault Sport)*

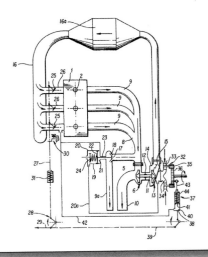

United States Patent [19]

Boudy

[11] Patent Number: 4,471,616

[45] Date of Patent: Sep. 18, 1984

[54] **DEVICE FOR REGULATING THE AIR SUPPLY OF AN INTERNAL COMBUSTION ENGINE**

[75] Inventor: **Jean-Pierre Boudy,** Mennecy, France

[73] Assignee: **Renault Sport,** Viry-Chatillon, France

[21] Appl. No.: **405,190**

[22] Filed: **Aug. 4, 1982**

[30] **Foreign Application Priority Data**

Mar. 29, 1982 [FR] France 82 05293

[51] Int. Cl.³ **F02B 37/00**

[52] U.S. Cl. **60/611;** 60/600; 415/160; 415/163

[58] Field of Search 60/600, 601, 611; 415/163, 160

[56] **References Cited**

U.S. PATENT DOCUMENTS

2,427,136 9/1947 Hagen 415/160

3,049,865	8/1962	Drayer	60/611
3,059,415	10/1962	Birmann	60/611
3,208,213	9/1965	Anderson	60/611
3,232,043	2/1966	Birmann	60/611
4,318,273	3/1982	Nohira	60/611

Primary Examiner—Douglas Hart
Attorney, Agent, or Firm—Oblon, Fisher, Spivak, McClelland & Maier

[57] **ABSTRACT**

In a device for regulating the air supply of an internal combustion engine supercharged by a turbo-compressor unit driven in rotation by the engine's exhaust, the intake of the rotating compressor is controlled by an intake regulation (or gating) system capable of reducing the compressive effect of the rotor of the compressor. Control elements of said regulation (or gating) system are connected with the accelerator linkage so as to close the regulation (or gating) system and reduce the compressive effect to the maximum degree when the accelerator moves toward the idling position of the engine.

7 Claims, 2 Drawing Figures

The Lotus 98T featured a further innovation for use during qualifying. An electric pump sprayed water into the front of the intercooler, using the cooling effect of its evaporation to enhance intercooler performance and deliver cooler inlet air and a denser air charge; the water flow was regulated to match boost pressure. As the spray was deemed unnecessary in a race, the reservoir, cleaned and sterilised, was used to supply the driver with drinking water.

Boost-control wastegate

As engine revs and exhaust velocities rise, so does the turbine speed of the turbocharger and, with it, boost pressure. Without control, this can lead ultimately to ever-spiralling, uncontrollable power outputs accompanied by destructive pre-ignition and detonation in the cylinders or surge and over-pressurisation in the inlet system. The boost level on each of the car's two turbochargers is therefore controlled by a wastegate, which is designed to bleed excess pressure from the exhaust manifold once the inlet air pressure reaches a pre-determined level.

Situated at the junction of the three exhaust-manifold branches, each wastegate is held in place by two clamps and contains a diaphragm that senses pressure. When boost pressure reaches a pre-set level, an electrically actuated, spring-loaded poppet valve is opened in order to allow exhaust gases to bypass the turbocharger, exiting via a separate exhaust tailpipe on each side of the car. Meanwhile, the main flow of the gases continues to power the turbocharger.

The boost level and wastegate settings are the prime means of controlling the car's fuel consumption during a race. The cockpit-mounted dial control contains five settings with '1' corresponding to 3.2 bar and '5' equating

LEFT After exiting the turbochargers, the exhaust gases are directed onto the rear aerodynamic diffuser to boost its efficiency. *(James Ward)*

to 4.0 bar, with the lower boost setting allowing better fuel consumption.

The dual-clamp fittings allow the wastegates to be rapidly changed, or removed entirely, during a qualifying session, although mechanics needed to wear thick insulated gloves to handle the ultra-hot components. When run without wastegates, for short, ultra-fast 'flying' qualifying runs, boost levels of up to 5.7 bar were recorded.

Cooling system

The two radiators, which cool both oil and water, are remotely mounted at the forward ends of the sidepods and connected to the engine block and cylinder heads by a combination of fixed aluminium pipes and flexible hoses. Produced by IPRA of Turin, they are fed by belt-driven external oil and water pumps mounted low at the rear of the engine block.

Airflow to each radiator enters the front of the sidepod via a thin mesh filter (to collect any debris) and is ducted into a wedge-shaped carbonfibre airbox, which accelerates the airflow before directing it through the cooling matrix from where it vents through exit ports on the outside edge of the sidepod. A small amount of the inlet air continues back through ducts beyond the radiator, to provide the cooling airflow for the turbocharger intercoolers.

The principal source of heat is the extreme temperature, over 1,100 degrees centigrade, developed in the combustion chambers. Extra-tight cylinder tolerances are critical to transmitting the heat from the piston crown, via the piston rings to the cylinder bores and liners, and into the coolant. Internal waterways within the cylinder block and heads enable the circulation of the coolant through the engine and back to the radiators, with a small header tank and pressure-relief cap mounted on the rear of the monocoque allowing replenishment if required.

Oil system

The engine and turbochargers utilise the same lubricating oil, pumped in a dry-sump system from the integral 11-litre oil tank at the rear of the monocoque. The oil is sucked from the tank and pressurised by the belt-driven external eccentric rotor-type pumps before being fed through internal engine oilways to the crankshaft, cylinder head and camshaft assemblies before being returned to the tank via the oil-cooling elements within the radiators. The system utilises a main pressure pump and three scavenge pumps, one to return oil to the tank and two for each of the turbochargers.

Additional oil ways feed areas such as piston-cooling galleries and the oil is transferred by armoured and heat-insulated external pipework to the turbocharger assemblies.

In a race, oil consumption typically would be up to four or five litres of the 11-litre capacity.

Renault's long-term partner, Elf Lubricants, was at the forefront of developing oils to meet the challenge of turbocharged installations. In addition to having to withstand the high temperatures and sheer forces of the engine and its combustion processes, the oils were also required to be of low viscosity to reduce frictional drag and aid distribution. This led to the development of some of the polymer-derived synthetic oils now used today in modern road cars.

Fuel system

Driven from the front of the crankshaft, a mechanical pump provides fuel pressure, with the fuel transferred via a 'common-rail' distribution system to low-pressure solenoid injectors. Single injectors per cylinder (supplied by Weber Marelli of Italy) were used on the Renault EF4 engine, while later EF15 engines had dual injectors per cylinder (supplied by Bosch of Germany) to aid efficiency and throttle response. The switch to the German manufacturer was made for commercial

BELOW A prominent plenum chamber on top of the engine feeds the inlet air to the electronically controlled fuel-injection system.
(James Ward)

While the static compression ratio of the engine may seem relatively low at 7.5:1, the multiplication factor created by the turbocharger boost in effect produces a compression ratio within the cylinders of in excess of 12:1, creating a combustion environment that requires high-octane fuel to prevent destructive pre-ignition. Throughout the development of the Renault turbo V6 engine, the Elf oil company was at the forefront of evolving fuel compounds to enable ever-higher levels of performance.

Elf chemists developed special fuel that still met FISA's 102 octane requirement, but provided the combustion characteristics of higher octane ratings. While BMW, working in conjunction with German chemical giants BASF and Wintershall, achieved the same aim by producing a purely synthetic fuel, Elf was proud of reaching almost the same levels of efficiency with a fuel that was technically closer to regular petrol.

Beginning with high-octane aviation fuel as a basis, the scientists began to use the aromatic compounds aniline and toluene. Ultimately toluene would make up over 80% of the fuel formulation, with the remainder of the content being used as a 'filler' to bring the octane level back down to the mandated maximum. This toluene fuel made a massive difference to throttle response as well as to ultimate performance. The distinctive smell of this fuel reminds anyone in its presence that toluene's primary domestic role is as the main constituent of paint thinners.

A further advantage of this fuel came from the fact that its greater density meant that an additional 10kg could be carried in the tank.

For race fans, meanwhile, there was one further benefit from the aggressive combustion. The 1.5-litre turbo cars of the 1980s were three times louder than their muted contemporaries today!

BELOW The Renault engine could sustain high boost pressure for only a limited time; engine failures were frequently catastrophic. *(John Townsend, F1 Pictures)*

reasons, as the company became a supplier to Renault road cars.

The fuel-injection system was controlled by a Renix (Renault-Bendix) electronic control unit that was later further developed in-house by engineers at Viry-Châtillon. Induction airflow from the turbochargers is stabilised in plenum chambers above the inlet tracts to balance the charged air prior to it entering the inlet tracts. To regulate the airflow, twin butterfly controls were chosen instead of throttle slides (as used on non-turbo racing engines) because the highly pressurised inlet air was found to cause excess friction and sticking throttles.

ABOVE The Renault Sport engine was one of the first to combine electronic fuel injection with coil-on-plug electronic ignition. *(Renault Sport)*

Transmission

Clutch

Power from the engine's crankshaft is transmitted to an AP 7¼in diameter clutch with a hydraulically actuated, two-piece pressure and friction plate mechanism. The slave cylinder for the hydraulic actuating system is mounted in unit with the release bearing, inside the Lotus-built magnesium alloy clutch housing at the rear of the engine.

The clutch unit comprises a steel flywheel, with intermediate and main pressure plates, working in conjunction with steel driven plates

LEFT The Lotus 97T and 98T both utilised similar Hewland-derived five-speed transmissions, although a six-speed version was developed during 1986. *(James Ward)*

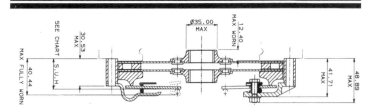

SINTERED TWIN PLATE
BACK TO BACK D/P
CP3174, CP3175

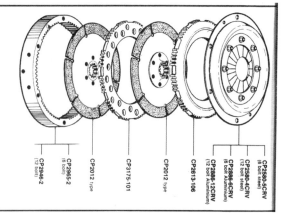

ABOVE A period AP clutch parts diagram shows the sintered-bronze friction components. *(AP)*

faced with a sintered-bronze friction material. The steel pressure plates are powered from the engine flywheel by teeth on both the flywheel and their perimeter, while the driven plates are attached to hubs on the splined gearbox input shaft. Even despite the power outputs involved, the AP clutch weighs a mere 4.45kg.

Due to the friction materials and the high levels of engine torque and potential heat build-up, the clutch cannot be slipped. From a driver's perspective, the clutch is either in or out, with the driver relying on engine torque, tyre slip and tractability created within the engine management system to get the car off the start line.

The AP clutch was almost the standard fit among Formula 1 teams of the mid-1980s.

Developed from the earlier units used on Cosworth DFV engines, it had thicker pressure plates and a more robust 12-bolt (rather than six-bolt) fitting, and was to prove effective and reliable even as turbo power outputs soared. The Coventry-based company had a long-standing relationship with Team Lotus, having first begun to supply friction materials, brakes and clutches to Formula 1 teams in 1967.

Differential
Ahead of the main gearbox and forming an integrated 'transaxle' unit between the clutch and gearbox housings, the differential unit features a Salisbury-type limited-slip crownwheel and pinion assembly. Drive to the rear hub units is via steel driveshafts

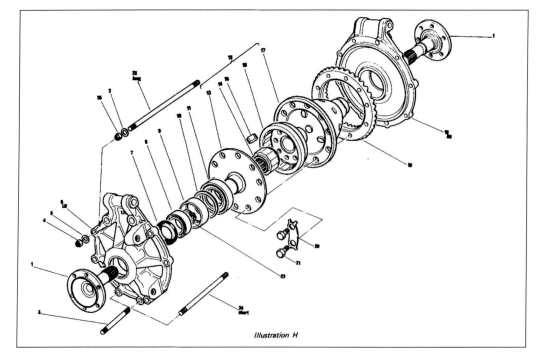

RIGHT Exploded view from a Hewland service manual shows the limited-slip differential components as item '12'.
(Hewland Transmissions)

Illustration H

through inner and outer Lobro steel constant-velocity joints.

Like most of the transmission components, the Salisbury-type differential was supplied by Hewland Engineering, a Berkshire-based engineering company established by Mike Hewland in 1957 to produce bespoke racing car gearboxes and transmission components.

The Salisbury unit limits asymmetric rotation of the two driveshafts, to prevent individual wheels spinning, by use of a stack of thin clutch discs on one of the driveshafts. Half of these are coupled to the driveshaft, the other half to the spider gear carrier in the differential. By increasing the pressure or pre-load on these clutches, the differential action is reduced.

The Salisbury system was used for the majority of races, although tests were carried out with Torsen torque-sensitive differentials using worm gears and spur gears to distribute power. ZF cam-and-pawl differentials were also used on occasion, their more aggressive action being better suited to tight street circuits.

Gearbox

A Lotus-designed cast-magnesium casing combines both the gearbox and differential housings, as well as acting as a structural chassis component incorporating the rear suspension wishbone, coil spring and damper pick-up points. It also contains a separate transmission oil tank of 5.5 litres capacity.

The transmission is driven from an extended gearbox input shaft, which runs from the clutch, through a tunnel in the oil tank and into the main gearbox. The transmission internals are based on proprietary Hewland DGB internals, which were derived from the original DG300 gearbox that Team Lotus first used in the Lotus 49 in 1967.

The in-line transmission features a conventional parallel mainshaft and layshaft design with three separate selector rods and forks for first and reverse gears, second and third, and fourth and fifth. The layshaft gears are removable via the end of the casing to allow ratios to be changed rapidly. A pull-rod assembly running down the right side of the unit, engine bay and cockpit connects the transmission to the manual H-configuration gear lever.

The transmission is lubricated by SAE 80 or SAE 90 oil, fed from the oil tank by a

LEFT Power is transmitted from the differential via steel driveshafts and Lobro constant-velocity joints. *(James Ward)*

ABOVE A Lotus-designed magnesium casting (with cast-in 'Lotus' identity) contains the gearbox and differential, and provides rear suspension pick-up points. *(Author)*

SIX-SPEED WOES

For the 1986 season, a new one-piece magnesium transaxle casing was introduced for the Lotus 98T into which a modified Hewland DGB assembly was incorporated, offering six forward speeds. Ayrton Senna, concerned about its potential reliability, declined to use it, remaining with the five-speed configuration. It proved a typically astute decision.

Team Lotus 'new boy' Johnny Dumfries was saddled with the development process, which rapidly turned sour when the transmission not only suffered mechanical failures but also displayed signs that the new casing was flexing, exacerbating the unreliability as the gears were not correctly meshing, and also potentially affecting the handling of the car. In addition, the problems with the six-speed gearbox meant that Dumfries frequently was unable to complete his testing and set-up programmes, meaning that he never truly got to demonstrate his potential in the Lotus 98T.

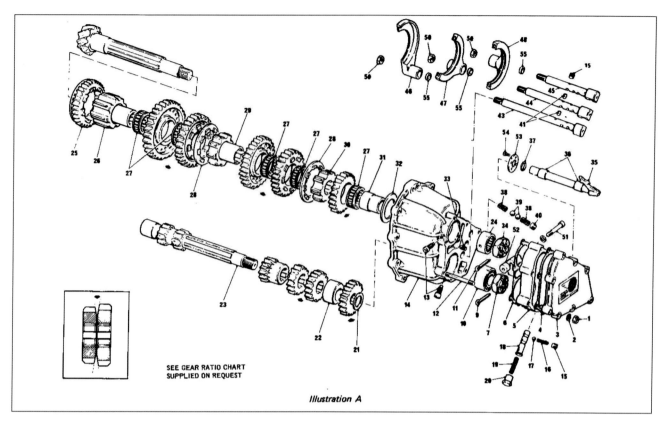

SEE GEAR RATIO CHART
SUPPLIED ON REQUEST

Illustration A

dedicated gear-driven oil pump at the rear of the gearbox casing.

The electronic revolution

Perhaps the fastest-moving area of progress in the era of the Lotus 97T and 98T was in the use of electronics. The advances extended from the development of new integrated digital systems controlling ignition and fuel injection to on-car data acquisition and the first portable computers in pit garages.

It should be remembered that when the Lotus 97T was being designed, it was still hand-drawn on a drawing board, while Ketteringham Hall echoed to the sound of mechanical typewriters. By the time the Lotus 98T was on the track the team was experimenting with the first live data links between the pits and the Team Lotus headquarters.

All electrical systems were powered by a lightweight Yuasa 12-volt gel battery located in the extreme nose of the car.

Combined ignition and injection

One area in which significant performance advances were made was engine management, with the development of integrated ignition and fuel injection with electronic control and mapping.

The original Renault EF4 engines had relied on electro-mechanical injection, with a cam on a

LEFT The combined electronic control of fuel injection and ignition systems pre-dated its use in modern road cars. *(Author)*

Kugelfischer metering unit controlled by signals from a basic microprocesser-based electronic control unit (ECU) handling five different control parameters. The distributor, sited in the valley of the engine's vee and driven from the cam belt, then transmitted low-tension electrical current to coil-on-plug ignition units on each cylinder. The supplier of these ignition units was first Weber-Marelli and then Bosch.

The distributor was subsequently replaced by a fully contactless digital system controlled by a Renix ECU, developed by a Renault-Bendix joint venture based in France's aerospace capital of Toulouse. The unit was designed to offer control of injection timing and duration, with integrated ignition control to ensure optimum mixture with minimum chance of destructive pre-ignition or detonation.

The main ECU 'box' is situated just behind the cockpit. It establishes ignition timing parameters, including crank position and engine speed, from a sensor on the front end of the crankshaft, as well as internal engine temperature, fuel pressure, fuel and air temperature, throttle position, inlet pressure, wastegate settings and boost levels, triggering low-voltage pulses from the ECU to the ignition amplifiers on the coil-on-plug units and activating the fuel injector solenoids on each respective cylinder to create the optimum combustion process.

The microprocessor within the ECU effectively controls two memory chips. A RAM (Random Access Memory) chip is utilised to handle calculations and fixed parameters, while a plug-in EPROM (Erasable Programmable Read-Only Memory) chip is programmed with the electronic mapping for all the engine parameters, initially developed from running engines on factory dynamometers. On the main engine ECU, these 'maps' would then be fine tuned at the track by using portable computers to reprogram the EPROM chips, which would be switched over in the ECU unit as required.

While trackside reprogramming was unlikely to result in any additional horsepower, its most significant advantage was in developing the

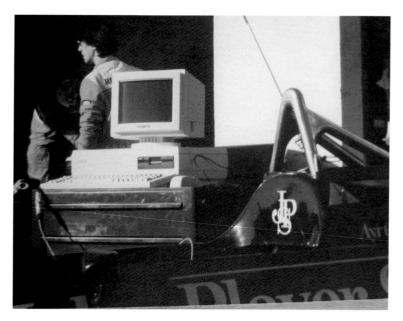

driveability of the engines, enhancing throttle response or engine torque at key parts of the circuit to suit driver requirements. In addition, as the teams all fought to optimise race fuel consumption, reprogramming of the EPROM chip allowed fine tuning of mixture levels to optimise fuel burn and maximise efficiency, running mixtures as lean as possible to the threshold of detonation.

In addition, on the Lotus 98T a fuel consumption indicator was developed. It displayed in the car's cockpit a fuel read-out, calculated in the pits based on known engine parameters and lap-time calculations and was updated on every lap by a radio signal as the car passed the pit wall. The information gained allowed the driver to make changes to driving style and tactics, to ensure finishing the race on the mandatory fuel allocation of 220 litres (1985) or 195 litres (1986).

Data-logging and telemetry

Initially data generated from the car's ECU system was stored within the unit's RAM board, for subsequent downloading when the car re-entered the pit garage. However, the spiralling amount of information rapidly began to outstrip memory capacity and dedicated data-logging systems were subsequently developed to allow more information and parameters to be handled.

Owing to capacity limitations, at first these data-logging systems merely recorded the maximum and minimum values for each parameter over a respective period. However, as memory capacity increased, it became possible to log the full spectrum of parameters against time, ultimately mapping them against the track location on any given lap.

In addition to engine parameters, data capture was extended to chassis evaluation, with brake-pedal force and steering sensors in the cockpit combining with load and temperature sensors on suspension and brakes to create a map of engine and chassis parameters as the car completed a lap.

Compared with modern data handling, things were still in their infancy. In 1985, Dr John Davis, the team's 'Computer Expert', described the set-up to *Lotus World* magazine: 'The team's requirements call for three computers.

One is here at Headquarters whilst two are used in the field. One of the latter units fits on the car and records data as it goes around. Then when the car comes into the pits, it transfers that information into the second unit on the pit counter. The other one that we have here is totally separate and is used for suspension characteristic calculations and other design works.'

Technology progressed rapidly and the data collected became more advanced, based on 3D chassis coordinates collated by a Scicon onboard computer mounted beneath the driver's seat. The accumulated data from this Scicon computer was downloaded into a Triple-X computer in the pits and later stored and analysed back at Ketteringham Hall.

By the start of the 1986 season, Team Lotus had announced a deal with Philips Business Systems to provide a wider range of electronic hardware. In addition to the installation of the first 'word processors' and an 'electronic internal mail system linked to telex' at Ketteringham Hall, Philips created a 'RaceData' system that used a telephone line for the first time, to provide a colour display on a television monitor at the team headquarters, showing lap times and other parameters direct from the circuit. The system was first used during initial shakedown testing of the Lotus 98T at Paul Ricard in France.

ABOVE The prominent radio antenna on Johnny Dumfries's car indicates early car-to-pits live data transmission in a 1986 Rio de Janeiro test session. *(John Townsend, F1 Pictures)*

BELOW This is how Team Lotus announced to the world their move into computer-driven technology, in 1986. *(Classic Team Lotus)*

Ayrton Senna

hn Player Speci

MICROM

12

Chapter Four

The driver's view

Only three drivers, Ayrton Senna, Elio de Angelis and Johnny Dumfries, drove the Lotus Renault 97T and 98T in anger and, given the pressures of the time, it is unsurprising that there are few immediate accounts of their views on what it was like to drive and race the cars in their day – but there are, thankfully, a few exceptions. In addition, Gary Ward, regular driver today of DT Performance's immaculate Lotus 98T, can also offer fascinating insights.

OPPOSITE Ayrton Senna's stature as one of the all-time greats was sealed during his three years with Team Lotus. *(John Townsend, F1 Pictures)*

Period descriptions

Interviewed in 1986 for *Lotus World*, the company's in-house magazine, Senna gave a hint at the sheer joy he found in pushing the Lotus 98T to its limit, not just in a grand prix but also in testing. Senna described his perfect day as: '…to have a sunny day, no wind, not too hot. Nice temperature. Exclusive track, maybe Silverstone. Silverstone is nice. Quick car, competitive car. Easy with the mechanics, everybody relaxed. And just drive it. A very quick car. A very powerful car, like the Lotus. Be with the engineers, with my team. And be able to improve it, drive it very quick, on the limit. Just, really drive it.'

Of course, the Brazilian's first victory in the Lotus 97T came in anything but the best of weather conditions. Even the indomitable Senna admitted that handling the Renault-powered turbo car in the torrential rain of the 1985 Portuguese Grand Prix stretched him to his limits. The situation was made worse by the fact that he had suffered mechanical failures in the Sunday morning warm-up session, requiring his car's gearbox to be replaced just ahead of the race.

Even though Senna at that time already had a grounding in Formula 1 behind him in the Toleman car and had claimed pole position in this race, only his second for Team Lotus, he was not afraid of telling Mike Doodson, *Motor* magazine's grand prix correspondent, of his wariness of the 97T prior to the race at Estoril: 'On the warming-up laps, the organisers gave us ten minutes' extra practice because of the conditions. I was absolutely lost. I had no idea how the car would behave on the track with so much water. Going from dry to wet with full tanks, what with having a new engine and a new gearbox, I was so slow that when I came back to the pits I couldn't even tell the team if the engine had any boost or anything. I hadn't dared to use any.'

Of course, come the race start, history records that Senna, who in his own words had 'tried a lil' bit harder than before', dominated proceedings to take victory by more than a minute!

Fuel-load effect

Compared with qualifying trim, the full fuel load at the start of a race made a car feel fundamentally different. Senna's team-mate for the 1986 season, Johnny Dumfries, described

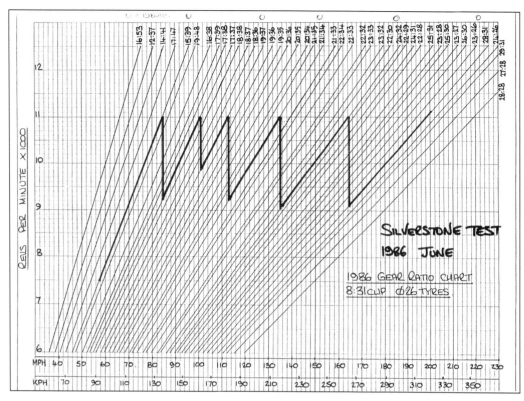

Handwritten chart annotations:

SILVERSTONE TEST
1986 JUNE

1986 GEAR RATIO CHART
8:31 C.W.P. ⌀26 TYRES

RPM PER MINUTE X 1000

(vertical axis values: 6, 7, 8, 9, 10, 11, 12)

MPH: 40 50 60 70 80 90 100 110 120 130 140 150 160 170 180 190 200 210 220 230

KPH: 70 90 110 130 150 170 190 210 230 250 270 290 310 330 350

LEFT Careful analysis of the gear ratios was vital. Here a test chart for Silverstone shows the car geared for well over 200mph.

the driving challenge in the 95T: 'The car felt horrible on full tanks: 200 litres of fuel is a lot of weight to be carrying, there's more chance of locking the wheels so you flat-spot a tyre, or turn in too late, or it's suddenly unbalanced and it all can go badly wrong. These cars were not kind on their tyres.'

Dumfries, in an interview with former Team Lotus press officer Johnny Tipler for his book, *Ayrton Senna: The Team Lotus Years*, described the challenge of handling the step-up in performance when driving the Lotus turbo car for the first time.

'The Formula 3000 cars were, in comparison, quite easy to drive. They only had 450bhp, they were pretty straightforward and were basically an overgrown F3 car with a DFV engine, positively crude by today's standards. The F1 cars at the time were enormously powerful and driving a turbo car required a different technique. They had much more downforce and the tyres had a lot more grip.'

Dumfries and his race engineer, Tim Densham, would spend many hours working as a team to formulate the set-up to get the best out of the car and its relatively narrow engine rev range. As Dumfries was principally using the six-speed gearbox, it meant a different planning

strategy to that of Senna and his race engineer Steve Hallam.

'It was very important to get the gear ratios right, preferably all the corners,' said Dumfries. 'If it was a circuit with a lot of corners, where you had to sacrifice one corner for another in terms of gear ratios, you'd make sure that the corner you'd got right was the one which would result in the best improvement in lap times. You

BELOW Dumfries's technique was to carry speed into the corner, then aim to be on full throttle by mid-corner, predicting the turbo lag. *(John Townsend, F1 Pictures)*

needed to get the entry right so that you could be on the power early enough to be carrying a lot of speed out of the corner.'

To minimise the effects of turbo lag, Dumfries's technique was to carry as much speed as possible into the corner. He would then aim to be on full throttle by the middle of the corner, predicting any throttle delay to allow the engine to be at full power to carry him out of the exit.

Blipping

With the turbo cars, Senna famously developed the technique of 'blipping' the throttle mid-corner. While some have speculated that this was a way to keep the turbocharger active and boost pressure high to aid throttle response, many others have pointed to it as a driving style learned in Senna's karting career.

By playing with the throttle and keeping the car teetering on the edge of adhesion on both the front and rear wheels, Senna could commit to a higher entry speed into corners. Team Lotus principal Peter Warr was quoted as

saying that only two drivers to his knowledge, both Lotus legends, were able to deliver this technique consistently – Senna and Jim Clark.

Warr also believed that another Senna attribute was that he would invariably push to the limit from the outset of a race while others 'played themselves in' during the opening laps. That is contradicted a little by an interview that Senna gave after finishing second in the 1985 Austrian Grand Prix, showing he had strong strategic acumen too.

'I know in this race a lot of cars are going to drop (out),' said Senna. 'The main thing is to keep going. Healthy, strong, not overdoing it, otherwise the car, the engine will give up. So I stay in mid-field for several laps, seeing how things settle down, then I start to push, others have tyre and engine trouble, I stay strong.'

Drama

A Senna contemporary, Gerhard Berger – Benetton, Ferrari and McLaren driver – perfectly summed up the drama, challenge and sheer heroics of the cars of the era.

'Going straight from F3 into one of those things, like I did… it seemed like the world had gone mad! I loved to have 5.5-bar boost, you had the throttle delay, you had to keep the boost up, you had to keep the wheels from spinning too much… and of course you had this unbelievable push forward.

'Some people say that they didn't enjoy the lack of instant engine response – but I loved that. I liked the fact that you arrived at a corner, and almost as soon as you turned in, you were on full throttle for the power you wanted 50 metres later! That was something, you know.

'You had to have the balls to go full throttle at a point where, if the power came too early, you were going to fly off the road. That was good fun – calculating where you had to push the throttle, and hoping you'd got it right! After that, anything else was going to be a disappointment, wasn't it?'

Former 1992 World Champion and former Team Lotus driver Nigel Mansell agrees. 'I look back now and think "did I really do that?" The cars were something else, the early turbo's power delivery was like a light switch, either on or off. You had to treat them with respect. We used to go flying into corners knowing if we got

RIGHT Nigel Mansell: 'I look back and think, did I really do that?' *(John Townsend, F1 Pictures)*

it wrong we would have a massive accident, so we respected the car and the corners. If we hit the kerb too hard, the feedback would actually tweak your wrists and you could damage yourself. We had to do physical training just to be able to hang on to the car – now drivers today with power steering can drive with a couple of fingers.'

JUST HOW FAST?

A demonstration of just how fast a Lotus-Renault turbo car is, both in contemporary terms and even today, was proven by an acceleration test carried out for *Motor* magazine by Elio de Angelis in 1985. The performance figures of his Lotus 97T were gained at a cold and misty Donington Park and then compared with those of the world's fastest sports car of the day, the Lamborghini Countach.

Owing to cold tyres, de Angelis took an apparently tardy two seconds to accelerate from a standstill to 40mph, but then 60mph was reached just a second later. After an earlier-than-normal gear-change to second at 62mph (the car was geared for 75mph at peak revs in first), the next change from second to third was made at 92mph, just 4.5 seconds after leaving the start line. Fourth gear was taken at 125mph, 6.0 seconds after the start, with fifth gear being attained at 154mph, 9.0 seconds from standstill,

ahead of a theoretical maximum speed of 175mph at 10,900rpm on the gearing of the day.

The Lamborghini reached 100mph from the standing start in 11.3 seconds, in comparison with 4.8 seconds for the Lotus 97T, but Team Lotus personnel claimed that their car had shown only a fraction of its potential. De Angelis apparently dismissed the acceleration as merely 'average'.

Peter Warr commented, 'If we could have done this on a hot day, with qualifying tyres and qualifying boost, it could have been a lot quicker.' Gérard Ducarouge added, 'We might be able to go 20mph faster on top speed.' Whatever the figures, it is an interesting thought that even with all the current technology, it is unlikely that a current Formula 1 car would accelerate any quicker.

Lotus 97T through the gears	
50–70mph	1.0s
60–80mph	1.0s
70–90mph	0.6s
80–100mph	0.8s
90–110mph	1.1s
100–120mph	1.2s
110–130mph	1.4s
120–140mph	1.6s
130–150mph	2.2s
140–160mph	3.0s

BELOW In 1985 Elio de Angelis demonstrated that a Lotus 97T would reach 100mph from a standing start in less than half the time of a Lamborghini Countach supercar. *(Classic Team Lotus)*

ACCELERATION COMPARISON		
	Lotus 97T	Lamborghini Countach
0–30mph	1.7s	2.2s
0–40mph	2.1s	2.9s
0–50mph	2.7s	3.6s
0–60mph	3.0s	4.8s
0–70mph	3.7s	6.0s
0–80mph	4.0s	7.5s
0–90mph	4.3s	9.3s
0–100mph	4.8s	11.3s
0–110mph	5.4s	13.8s
0–120mph	6.0s	17.4s
0–130mph	6.8s	
0–140mph	7.6s	
0–150mph	9.0s	
0–160mph	10.6s	

RIGHT Mastering the art of the perfect start was critical with the turbo cars' power characteristics and this sequence shows Senna doing just that, beating Piquet off the line in the 1986 French Grand Prix, with Dumfries making up ground midfield. *(John Townsend, F1 Pictures)*

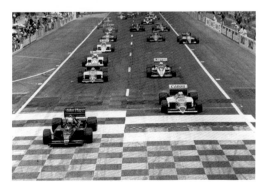

The perfect start

In a contemporary interview, Johnny Dumfries gave his take on achieving the perfect racing start in the 98T.

'As the lights went to red, I would depress the throttle slowly to the point of 12,000rpm. Then when I had it hovering there, I'd start to ease back on the clutch. You'd always be on the verge of jumping the start really, but you were in a sort of state of hyper-awareness. I'd always go straight for the middle of the row in front of me, I think if I had made that I'd have gained a minimum of two places, and sort it out from there.'

Driving a Lotus-Renault turbo car today

Gary Ward has probably amassed more laps in a Lotus-Renault Formula 1 car than any other driver apart from Ayrton Senna, Johnny Dumfries, Nigel Mansell and Elio de Angelis. Ward is the demonstration driver of the DT Performance Lotus 98T, chassis 04, the last-ever Lotus-Renault turbo car, used by Senna in the 1986 Australian Grand Prix. Patrick Morgan of DT Performance restored the car to absolutely original specification, creating an immaculate, time-warp machine.

A former international karting champion, Formula 3, Formula 3000 and Euroboss Formula 1 racer, young driver mentor and test driver for Honda's NSX turbo Le Mans cars, Ward has demonstrated 98/4 in recent years at many venues, including Goodwood, Silverstone, Brands Hatch and many of Europe's top grand prix circuits, such as Barcelona and Spa, in support of the Renault World Series.

'It's an incredible piece of kit,' says Gary. 'The first time you see it, it just draws the eye

with that black and gold livery, that aggressive stance. Then there's the noise. It sounds fantastic and I just love the smell of the toluene fuel mix!

'When you get in it, compared with a modern Formula 1 car, it's surprising how exposed you feel. You sit a long way forward, with your feet well ahead of the axle line. In later cars the driver was moved backwards for safety, more to the middle of the car. In the Lotus you really feel you are well out front, with that amazing engine behind you. That feeling of exposure is the same when you're on the track. In modern single-seaters the front wheels dominate your lines of vision, but in the Lotus they're further apart so your view of the track ahead – and your feeling of exposure – is that much greater.

'Unlike a lot of later cars, the cockpit is surprisingly comfortable. It's completely authentic, with Ayrton's carbonfibre seat and Ayrton's steering wheel, and with seat belts, pedal positions and gear-lever position all designed to fit him. Everything is well laid out and easy to operate, and I'm perfectly comfortable in it. Unlike some Formula 1 cars I've driven, the Lotus 98T is remarkably user-friendly.'

The Lotus 98T remains, as Gary gleefully admits, as fast as ever.

'The acceleration just keeps going and going. It's a very smooth engine too. It has much less vibration than, say, a Cosworth DFV. The engine has masses of torque and not as much turbo lag as you might expect.

'We run the car at about 4.0 bar of boost, which is pretty much as it raced. When we were demonstrating the car at Spa, we were using fourth and fifth gears through Eau Rouge and, despite having a high-downforce setting on the wings, we were still hitting the rev limiter in top gear, probably close to 200mph, so horsepower is clearly never going to be a problem!

'Getting cleanly off the start line under the pressure of a race start would have been a challenge in the day. It's not too bad if you use a constant start technique: stabilise the revs at 5,000rpm, drop the clutch (no slip) then balance the throttle so you don't get wheelspin, or you'll lose all the boost when you change from first to second. The car would rev to 11,000 in race trim, but we use 9,500 or 10,000 today.'

Out of deference to the precious machinery, Gary uses the clutch to reduce loads on the gearbox during both up and down changes, occasionally using downshifts to help the braking effort into slower corners.

'You've really got to watch the brake temperatures. The carbon brakes need to be used aggressively to keep their temperatures in the right operating range. If you let them get cool, you suddenly get that horrible feeling you're just not going to stop!

'The car handles well, generates loads of downforce. It's a handful, but it's still a car you drive by feel.

'I just feel immensely privileged to be able to drive it on some of the best circuits in the world. One highlight had to be an early-morning demonstration on the Barcelona grand prix circuit, running with René Arnoux in a Renault Sport F1 car. We were both pushing on and apparently our rear wing vortices were leaving vapour trails like a pair of jet fighters!

'Driving the 98T leaves me with huge admiration for Senna and Dumfries. Full-boost qualifying must have been awesome; just imagine going out of the pitlane with 500 horsepower more than you had before in the same car. But it's how those drivers actually raced that impresses me. Handling one of these cars, with no driver aids, no power steering and a manual, H-pattern gear-change, for 80 laps of a grand prix – that would have been pretty hard work.'

ABOVE Gary Ward demonstrating the Lotus 98T at Goodwood Festival of Speed. *(Courtesy of Patrick Morgan)*

BELOW As demonstration driver of Lotus 98T/4, Gary Evans has modern-day experience of the 30-year-old technology. *(Courtesy of Patrick Morgan)*

Chapter Five

The engineer's view

What was it like to be a race engineer during the time of the Lotus 97T and 98T, with their awesomely powerful turbo engines, their new levels of sophistication in composite construction and aerodynamics, and their proliferation of innovative electronic systems? This chapter looks at the role in all of its aspects, from building the cars, through all phases of their operation at grands prix, to the all-important business of testing.

OPPOSITE Ayrton Senna with crew prior to a qualifying run at Monza in 1986. For a race the tank would be filled to the brim, but for qualifying, when just a small amount of fuel was needed, the unnecessary space was taken up by ping-pong balls. Seen attending to the car are, from left to right: Steve Hallam (with cap), Paul Diggins, Colin Watts (with fuel can), Nigel Stepney (placing funnel), Bob Dance and Richard Hodgson. *(John Townsend, F1 Pictures)*

By modern Formula 1 standards, Team Lotus would be viewed as a tiny operation. Even at the peak of the turbo era, no more than 60 staff worked at the team's Ketteringham Hall headquarters, handling not just the design and build of the cars, but also PR, marketing, logistics, personnel and transport – and, of course, ensuring that the team was up to date with the ever-changing FISA regulations.

It should be remembered, too, that the team was operating in an era where laptop computers, e-mails and the internet were unknown. It was only in the spring of 1986 that the first 'word-processor computers' were delivered to the team's headquarters, and 'telefax' machines were still in their infancy. It is almost inconceivable today that the logistics, transportation and planning for shipping cars, engines and personnel around the world, for a 16-race calendar starting in Brazil and ending in Australia, was co-ordinated using typed memos, telephone calls, telex messages and posted letters!

Race team mechanics

Building and running the race cars was a task entrusted to a group of mechanics numbering fewer than 20, under the control of chief mechanic Bob Dance. Bob, who today still prepares Lotus grand prix cars for Clive

LEFT **Pre-radio, hard-wired communications required the engineers to physically plug in to talk to the driver in the pitlane.** (John Townsend, F1 Pictures)

Chapman and Classic Team Lotus, jokes that in 1960 Clive's father tried to talk him out of joining the Formula 1 team.

'I asked Colin Chapman if I could switch from the components and developments department at Lotus to the race team, but Colin said, "Don't do that, it's a dead-end job." He was right, because here I am all these years later still doing it!'

Bob works at Classic Team Lotus alongside Chris Dinnage, the team manager there. Chris recalls how, as a 21-year-old, he was offered his 'big break' by Dance in 1983 after working for a year on Formula 1 suspension sub-assemblies.

'We were in transition,' says Dinnage. 'We'd abandoned the normally aspirated Cosworth engines and the team realised that with the new turbocharged Renault-powered cars, their complexity meant we needed three mechanics per car instead of two. Three of us – Jonathan Woodward, Colin Watts and me – were drafted into the race team perhaps 18 months before we normally would have been. Usually you would have done a year on sub-assemblies and another year on the test team before you were considered for the race team.

'The chief mechanic was really a man manager. He was in charge of everybody and everything. He even told us what time we had to get up in the morning. Below him, the key people on each car were the number one mechanic and the two guys who worked with him. They were the ones who produced the car, and they were responsible for the reliability and continuity.'

Dinnage's role was to help build the race cars at the factory for both drivers then, at the track, to look after the team's spare or T-car. In 1985 this was shared between Elio de Angelis and Ayrton Senna, but in 1986 it was almost exclusively for the Brazilian's use.

For the 1985 and 1986 seasons, Steve Hallam was the race engineer on Senna's race car supported by Paul Simpson, Tony Fletcher and Jon Woodward, while in the successive years the sister car was looked after by mechanics Paul Diggins and Colin Watts, under the control of race engineer Tim Densham (now a designer at Renault F1) and number one mechanic Nigel Stepney.

Stepney, who was tragically killed in a road

ABOVE **The close relationship between Ayrton Senna and race engineer Steve Hallam was a feature of the Brazilian's time with Team Lotus.** (John Townsend, F1 Pictures)

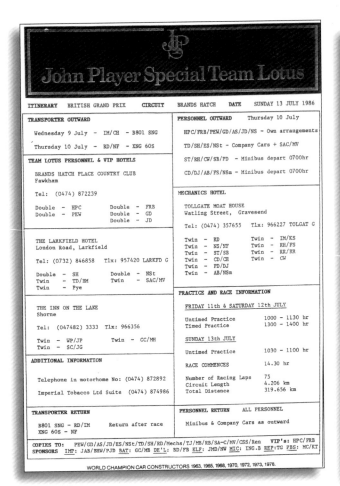

John Player Special Team Lotus

| ITINERARY | BRITISH GRAND PRIX | CIRCUIT | BRANDS HATCH | DATE | SUNDAY 13 JULY 1986 |

TRANSPORTER OUTWARD

Wednesday 9 July – IM/CH – B801 SNG

Thursday 10 July – RD/NF – XNG 60S

TEAM LOTUS PERSONNEL & VIP HOTELS

BRANDS HATCH PLACE COUNTRY CLUB
Fawkham

Tel: (0474) 872239

Double – HPC   Double – FRB
Double – PEW   Double – GD
                Double – JD

THE LARKFIELD HOTEL
London Road, Larkfield

Tel: (0732) 846858 Tlx: 957420 LARKFD G

Double – SH   Double – NSt
Twin – TD/BM   Twin – SAC/MV
Twin – Pye

THE INN ON THE LAKE
Shorne

Tel: (047482) 3333 Tlx: 966356

Twin – WP/JP   Twin – CC/MH
Twin – SC/JG

ADDITIONAL INFORMATION

Telephone in motorhome No: (0474) 872892

Imperial Tobacco Ltd Suite (0474) 874986

TRANSPORTER RETURN

B801 SNG – RD/IM   Return after race
XNG 60S – NF

PERSONNEL OUTWARD   Thursday 10 July

HPC/FRB/PEW/GD/AS/JD/NS – Own arrangements

TD/SH/ES/NSt – Company Cars + SAC/MV

ST/RH/CW/SB/PD – Minibus depart 0700hr

CD/DJ/AB/NSm – Minibus depart 0700hr

MECHANICS HOTEL

TOLLGATE MOAT HOUSE
Watling Street, Gravesend

Tel: (0474) 357655   Tlx: 966227 TOLGAT G

Twin – RD   Twin – IM/KS
Twin – NS/NF   Twin – RH/FS
Twin – ST/SB   Twin – RR/RR
Twin – CD/CH   Twin – CW
Twin – PD/DJ
Twin – AB/NSm

PRACTICE AND RACE INFORMATION

FRIDAY 11th & SATURDAY 12th JULY

Untimed Practice   1000 – 1130 hr
Timed Practice   1300 – 1400 hr

SUNDAY 13th JULY

Untimed Practice   1030 – 1100 hr

RACE COMMENCES   14.30 hr

Number of Racing Laps   75
Circuit Length   4.206 km
Total Distance   319.656 km

PERSONNEL RETURN   ALL PERSONNEL

Minibus & Company Cars as outward

COPIES TO: PEW/GD/AS/JD/ES/NSt/TD/SH/RD/Mechs/TJ/MB/RB/SA–C/MV/CSS/Ren   VIP's: HPC/FRB
SPONSORS IMP: JAB/BHW/PJD BAT: GC/MB DE'L: BD/FB ELF: JMD/NW MIC: ING.B REP:TG PBS: MC/KT

WORLD CHAMPION CAR CONSTRUCTORS 1963, 1965, 1968, 1970, 1972, 1973, 1978.

TEAM LOTUS INTERNATIONAL

BUILD SPECIFICATION

CHASSIS NO: 98/4   DRIVER: AYRTON

CIRCUIT: BRANDS   EVENT: GP   DATE: 11,12,13 JULY 1986

ENGINE: GEARBOX: P&B 14 – 15   C.W.P. 8,31

	1st	2nd	3rd	4th	5th
INITIAL RATIOS:	15:34	16:38	20:36	22:32	23:27

SETTINGS:	INITIAL		FINAL	
	F	R	F	R
SPRINGS	BLUE/WHITE	YELLOW/GRN		
BARS: TYPE	⌀20,6	⌀15		
POSN.	ADJ	MID		
DAMPERS	BAS3 1604	BAS3 1610		
BUMP/REBOUND	48–72	08–48		
RUBBER/PACKER	SID/C+OP	SID/C+OP		
BRAKES: CALS/DISCS	BREMBO/SCP	BREMBO/SCP		
PADS	SEP	SEP		
M/CYLS	⌀10,6	⌀22		
DUCTS	U.HUBE	U.HUBE		

	1st	2nd	3rd	4th	5th
FINAL RATIOS:					

NOTES:-
1. F.WINGS , + 15% 41+6L
2. DEFLECTORS
3. R.WINGS : T98 +14L +LOW INCID + MAX LOW FLAP

---

accident in May 2014, went on from Team Lotus to join Benetton and then Ferrari, where he was chief mechanic throughout Michael Schumacher's World Championship-dominating era.

'Nigel taught me how to build reliable racing cars,' said Dinnage. 'He instilled that into the Italians too. When he left them in 2007, they stopped winning.'

Practice and qualifying

Typically, around 18 to 20 team personnel, including team management, would travel to races, with additional people, including VIP guests, PR staff and sponsors, added to the list as required. A detailed 'movements sheet' would be typed up in the Ketteringham Hall offices, photocopied and distributed to all personnel as required. Except for a 'home' race, this would be accompanied by information on flights, rental cars, hotels and other travel details as required.

The cars carried their own paperwork to each event. Before leaving the Team Lotus workshops,

each car would be checked against its build inspection, which included key parameters such as gear ratios, spring and damper types and settings, castor and camber settings, brake cylinder types and air ducts, and aerodynamic configuration. The car would also be drained of fuel and the water injection tank emptied, then weighed before leaving the workshop.

The team transporter and motorhome would typically arrive at a track on a Wednesday afternoon, to allow the pit garage and equipment to be unloaded and set up, prior to the cars being scrutineered on the Thursday. On arrival at the track the dimensional checks on the cars would be repeated in case any units had 'settled' during transport. The car was then reweighed, this time with a pre-calculated amount of fuel on board.

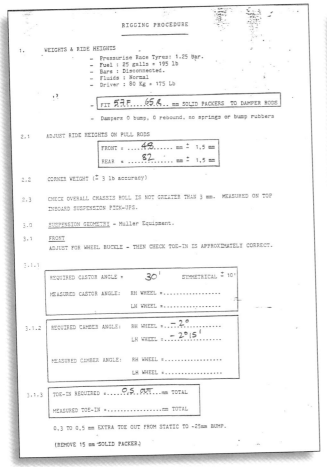

RIGGING PROCEDURE

1.   WEIGHTS & RIDE HEIGHTS
- Pressurise Race Tyres: 1.25 bar.
- Fuel : 25 galls = 195 lb
- Bars : Disconnected.
- Fluids : Normal
- Driver : 80 Kg = 175 Lb

- FIT 57.F..... 65.R.. mm SOLID PACKERS TO DAMPER RODS

- Dampers 0 bump, 0 rebound, no springs or bump rubbers

2.1   ADJUST RIDE HEIGHTS ON PULL RODS

FRONT = ...43...... mm ± 1,5 mm

REAR = ...82...... mm ± 1,5 mm

2.2   CORNER WEIGHT (± 3 lb accuracy)

2.3   CHECK OVERALL CHASSIS ROLL IS NOT GREATER THAN 3 mm. MEASURED ON TOP
    INBOARD SUSPENSION PICK-UPS.

3.0   SUSPENSION GEOMETRY - Muller Equipment.

3.1   FRONT
    ADJUST FOR WHEEL BUCKLE - THEN CHECK TOE-IN IS APPROXIMATELY CORRECT.

3.1.1

REQUIRED CASTOR ANGLE =   30'   SYMMETRICAL ± 10'

MEASURED CASTOR ANGLE: RH WHEEL =...................
                   LH WHEEL =...................

3.1.2   REQUIRED CAMBER ANGLE: RH WHEEL =..-2°..........
                           LH WHEEL =..-2°15'........

MEASURED CAMBER ANGLE: RH WHEEL =...................
                           LH WHEEL =...................

3.1.3   TOE-IN REQUIRED =.....0.5..OUT....mm TOTAL

MEASURED TOE-IN =.................mm TOTAL

0,3 TO 0,5 mm EXTRA TOE OUT FROM STATIC TO -25mm BUMP.

(REMOVE 15 mm SOLID PACKER)

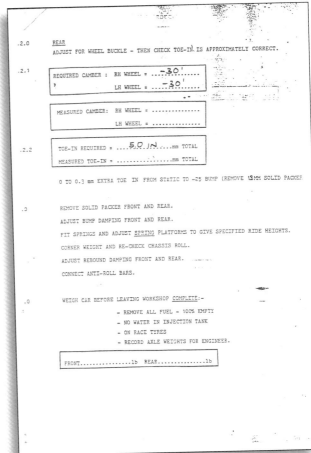

.2.0   REAR
    ADJUST FOR WHEEL BUCKLE - THEN CHECK TOE-IN IS APPROXIMATELY CORRECT.

.2.1

REQUIRED CAMBER : RH WHEEL = ...-30'
                  LH WHEEL = ...-30'

MEASURED CAMBER: RH WHEEL = ...
                  LH WHEEL = ...

.2.2   TOE-IN REQUIRED = ...5.0.IN......mm TOTAL

MEASURED TOE-IN = ...mm TOTAL

0 TO 0.3 mm EXTRA TOE IN FROM STATIC TO -25 BUMP (REMOVE 15MM SOLID PACKER

.0   REMOVE SOLID PACKER FRONT AND REAR.

ADJUST BUMP DAMPING FRONT AND REAR.

FIT SPRINGS AND ADJUST SPRING PLATFORMS TO GIVE SPECIFIED RIDE HEIGHTS.

CORNER WEIGHT AND RE-CHECK CHASSIS ROLL.

ADJUST REBOUND DAMPING FRONT AND REAR.

CONNECT ANTI-ROLL BARS.

.0   WEIGH CAR BEFORE LEAVING WORKSHOP COMPLETE:-
- REMOVE ALL FUEL - 100% EMPTY
- NO WATER IN INJECTION TANK
- ON RACE TYRES
- RECORD AXLE WEIGHTS FOR ENGINEER.

FRONT................lb   REAR...............lb

A standard Formula 1 schedule for all events was mandated by the FIA and FISA over the three days of a grand prix weekend on Friday, Saturday and Sunday. The only exception to this occurred at Monaco, where for historical reasons the initial track running was moved forward to the Thursday, to allow the traditional food market to take place on the Friday morning.

On Friday mornings, the first one and a half hours of track time, between 8.00am and 9.30am, was allocated to the first free practice session, followed by the first of two hour-long qualifying sessions between 11.00am and noon. Unlike current Formula 1 timetables, there was no 'shoot-out' format and drivers could run as often as they liked, although in practical terms the characteristics of the turbocharged cars meant that they were restricted to a handful of three-lap runs, with a warm-up lap and a cooling-down lap sandwiching a one-lap 'flyer'.

'We used to change the turbochargers after every qualifying run, because the turbos would get so stressed that they were finished after just one lap,' recalled Steve Hallam when interviewed for a *Club Lotus* article. 'The mechanics needed half an hour to change them, so the qualifying laps had to be a minimum of half an hour apart.

'The turbos would glow red-hot, and the mechanics had these massively thick asbestos

BELOW Practice and qualifying involve long hours spent checking and replacing frequently inaccessible components. *(John Townsend, F1 Pictures)*

gloves to handle them and undo the bolts. And they'd be clicking and pinging as they cooled off. When you took the body off, the air around them was literally sparking as they were so hot. The boys would be sweating and you'd hear the sizzle as the moisture dripped on to the turbo.'

During qualifying, where a full tank of fuel was not required, the necessary fuel volume was calculated and then ping-pong balls equating to the remaining volume were placed in the tank to occupy the spare capacity. This meant that it was not necessary to measure fuel quantity during the pressures of a qualifying session.

QUALIFYING DOMINATION

Ayrton Senna's qualifying pace in the Lotus 98T in the opening three races of the 1986 season literally caused sparks to fly up and down the pitlane. Observers from rival teams were increasingly concerned that the titanium skid plates on the underside of the Lotus were in contact with the track far more than was the case with other cars.

Was there some unknown flexibility allowing the supposed flat-bottomed car to side-step the regulations? Even though there was no official protest, FISA scrutineers inspected the Team Lotus cars with ride-height and suspension-deflection tests at the San Marino Grand Prix, along with cars from three other teams – and they could find nothing amiss.

Throughout the season, Senna's rivals continued to level allegations concerning his qualifying pace to such an extent that Team Lotus eventually made a public statement in the form of an ultimatum, issued at the Mexican Grand Prix in October. After stating the technical details, the statement read: 'While Colin Chapman would have been proud of and enjoyed the controversy surrounding a car carrying the name Lotus, the defamatory and derogatory statements must now either: – (1) Stop or (2) Be supported by an official protest as provided for in the Sporting Regulations or (3) Be answered by the persons making them when Team Lotus will be forced to seek recompense for the damage to its reputation.'

It is noteworthy that even though Senna went on ultimately to claim eight pole positions with the 98T that year, there was never any confirmation of any impropriety. Today it can be assumed that the performance was purely the blend of aerodynamic efficiency, the raw power of the Renault EF15 engine – and Senna's brilliance.

LEFT The press statement issued by Team Lotus at the 1986 Mexico Grand Prix regarding rumours surrounding qualifying domination.

Although the team was developing car-to-pit radio communications, the technology was still in its infancy in 1986, so most data transfer and communication was 'hard-wired', with engineers and technicians 'plugging-in' to sockets on the sidepods and cockpit of the car when it arrived in the pits. Renault's Bruno Maudit would connect engine data cables while Lotus 'boffin' John Davis would affix additional data-logging cables. For voice communications with the driver, particularly the team's number one, Senna, there was a clear pecking order for those lining up to speak.

'First Peter Warr would plug in,' Dinnage recalls, 'then his race engineer Steve Hallam, then the Renault engineer Bruno Maudit – and then Gérard Ducarouge would plug in for his two Francs' worth!'

During free practice and qualifying sessions, lap charts would be kept, hand-written on a pre-printed log sheet that also carried, at its head, all of the principal engine and chassis settings for quick reference. If any changes were made to any of the car's parts or parameters, these too would be logged for future reference.

Post-qualifying, as the drivers and race engineers went into debrief meetings, Bob Dance and the number-one mechanics on each car would supervise work done according to a pre-prepared checklist, with the mechanics measuring components for wear, checking for cracks or other damage, and replacing components or assemblies – including engines and gearboxes – that had reached the end of their working lives.

ABOVE A crowded pitlane scene with tyres being changed prior to a qualifying run; among the personnel is chief mechanic Bob Dance, at the left-front wheel. (*John Townsend, F1 Pictures*)

BELOW Before access was restricted to essential personnel only on safety grounds, the pitlane – this is Mexico in 1986 – could prove chaotic. (*Classic Team Lotus*)

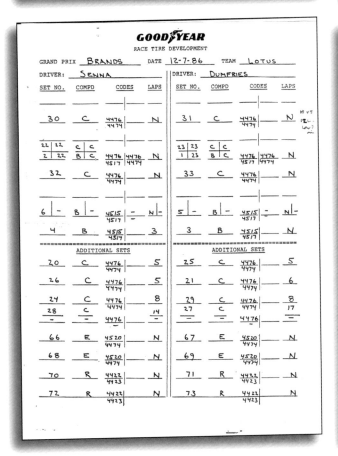
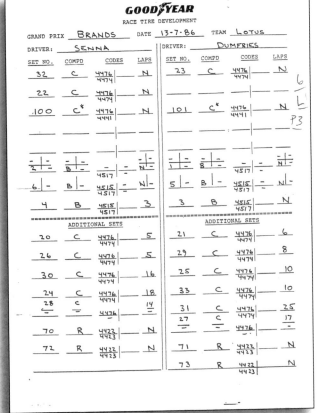

With the work completed late on Friday evening or even in the small hours of Saturday morning, the pit garage would be secured and the mechanics would head off for a few hours' rest, before the entire process would be repeated. An early 6.00am start was required on Saturday ahead of the second free practice session between 8.00am and 9.30am, and a second hour-long qualifying session between 11am and noon.

A typical working week for a Team Lotus mechanic was at least 70 hours. By contrast, Renault's engine mechanics were constrained by French labour laws and working-time directives. To the Lotus mechanics' annoyance, a Renault technician was required to be on hand whenever a newly installed engine was fired up, and time was often wasted as they waited for the elusive man to appear.

Despite the best efforts of Bruno Maudit, Renault's urbane and bilingual liaison engineer, Bob Dance diplomatically referred to some of the Renault technicians as 'temperamental' and could often barely hide his frustration.

'I liked to get on, get done and go,' says Dance, 'whereas they would shuffle about, take their time and not get stuck into it. If you tried to get it speeded up, all you actually did was slow them down.'

Race day

Sunday morning also offered little potential for rest. Between Saturday afternoon and Sunday the cars were reconfigured with engines and gearboxes changed for longer-lifed and race-optimised units, while items used only in qualifying, such as the water injection for the intercoolers, were removed. The cars in race trim were then allocated a further 30-minute

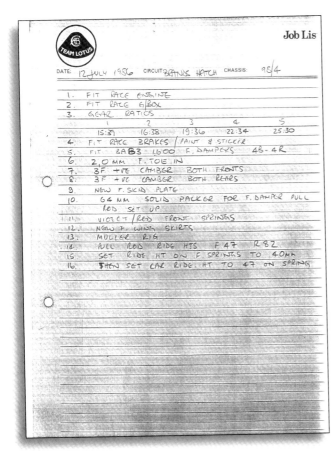

'warm-up' session between 8.30 and 9.00am, allowing a maximum of three hours to overcome any snags before the cars headed to the starting grid for the 12.30pm race start.

Prior to the start, a final checklist would be run through, including fuel level, all vital fluids, tyres, tyre compounds and tyre pressures, along with checks on the cars' electronic systems and finally a late 'spanner check' to ensure that all the panels and bodywork were secure. Once on the grid, there was little more to be done other than to ensure that the air starter with associated air bottle was on hand to start the engine.

With the race underway, the pit wall was a focal point. The race engineers would not only monitor track position and strategy, and pass information to the drivers by pit boards, but they would also keep a detailed lap chart, recording manually, with stopwatches, not just all laps by the two JPS-Lotus cars but also the performance of key rivals at each stage of the race.

There was often some hidden hilarity at the sight of the tall, erect figure of Peter Warr perched on the pit wall in a folding aluminium garden chair. However, Warr was happy to point out that his choice of seat was comfortable, light in weight, easily portable and, above all, cheap!

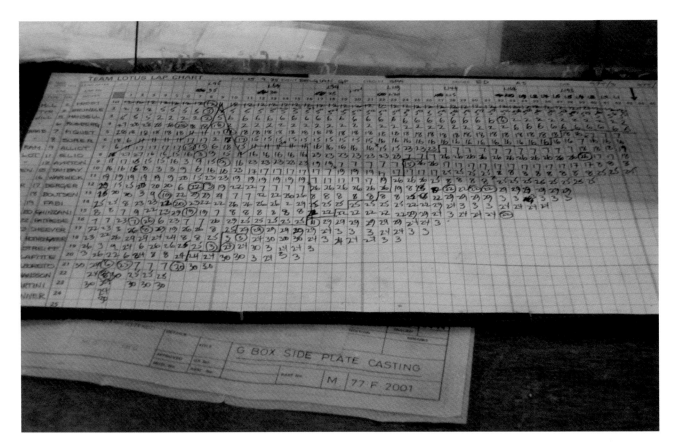

There was also mirth at the rain-soaked Belgian Grand Prix at Spa in 1985, when Warr had the team create a waterproof plastic cover to protect his lap charts. Dubbed 'the fish tank', this had been decorated, anonymously, with a couple of cut-out goldfish by the time the team manager arrived on the pit wall as the cars left the start line on their warm-up lap. Warr had the last laugh, of course, for his notes recorded that Senna crossed the line 28 seconds ahead of Nigel Mansell to score his second grand prix victory.

The race, of course, is a time of high tension for the team as a whole, but for many of the mechanics it is actually their one chance to relax, with the significant exception of the periods around the pre-selected pit-stop windows. While in-race refuelling was not allowed, a quick (sub-10 second) tyre stop could make the difference, then as now, between victory and defeat. The mechanics were always on standby, however, in case an unexpected drama such as a puncture were to force the car to make an unscheduled stop.

Late in the race some of the team personnel would be delegated to start loading non-essential equipment into their transport cases for loading into the transporter once the chequered flag had fallen.

Once the race was over, there would be a short engineering debrief before the drivers and senior engineers left the circuit, and while the cars underwent post-race scrutineering. Then it was a case of final packing and loading before leaving the circuit. Such was the speed of post-race loading that at a European grand prix, where all equipment came by road, it was considered very bad form if the transporter had not departed by 10.00pm.

Once back at the factory at the start of the following week, the mechanics would be greeted by an engineering sheet. Prepared by the tireless Warr on the evening after the race, it specified a list of tasks to be completed on each car, ahead of its next outing.

Testing

In comparison with the heavily restricted testing of today's Formula 1 cars, the situation during the 1980s was very open and regular test sessions were used to verify engine,

ABOVE **The lap chart Warr kept at Spa still survives in the Classic Team Lotus archives, showing Senna's Lotus 97T heading for victory.** *(Author)*

chassis and aerodynamic changes with the theoretical calculations. Team Lotus was well placed to take full advantage of this.

Some testing could be carried out on the team's doorstep, at the Lotus Cars factory at Hethel, where part of the former wartime airfield on which the factory is located had been turned into a twisting test track. If higher speeds and longer straights were required, Snetterton was less than ten miles away.

With the introduction of tighter safety

requirements for testing following Elio de Angelis's fatal accident while testing for Brabham in May 1986, Lotus began to join other teams at group 'test days' at tracks such as Silverstone and Hockenheim, a situation that also allowed more cost-effective access to tyre supplies from Goodyear. At the start of each new season, testing took place in Rio de Janeiro, giving access to better weather than the European winter and allowing the teams to control costs by early shipping of some equipment that they would subsequently use at the first race of the season.

As for a race weekend, a detailed worksheet would show the key parameters to be tested and there would be meticulous monitoring of the resultant lap times and 'cornering times' over key sections of the lap. These would then be analysed in conjunction with the digital data from the car's electronics. At a test where there would be frequent changes of components such as springs, these would be colour-coded, allowing quick reference to the specifications after the test.

BELOW A typical memo from team manager Peter Warr, outlining the requirements for a test at Brands Hatch. (Courtesy of Patrick Morgan)

CIRCULATION	SUBJECT	ISSUED BY
GD/MBO/SH/TD/RV/RB/PH/RD/ INSP/COMP/FAB/WINGS/PAT/ M/C / S/ASSY /G'BOX/R & D/ 98/1 / 98/2 / 98/3 / 98/4 cc PEW	Job List 98/4	Peter Warr **DATE** 20th August 1986 **SHEET No.**

Budapest Practice miles:	194 m
Budapest Race miles:	234 m
Zeltweg Practice miles:	74 m
Zeltweg Race miles:	114 m
Total miles to date:	1496 m
CWP miles – pract. g/box:	268 m
CWP Miles – Race g/box	114 m

Car is to run on Wednesday at Brands Hatch to test the Zeltweg Race Engine. Car is to run with same engine/intercooler/radiator/fuel system

JOBS FOR BRANDS HATCH

1. Overhaul front suspension and Uprights
2. Fit new or overhauled dampers F & R;   Front - BA53 1604,   Rear - BA53 1610
3. Overhaul practice g/box and fit new CWP
4. Inspect visually and check practice rear suspension
5. Overhaul Practice Rear Uprights and Driveshafts
6. Rig car
7. Settings and Ratios as sheet

OTHER JOBS

1. Pressure check and steam clean Intercoolers
2. Steam clean Radiators
3. Fit Monza Race Engine (after Brands)
4. Inspect Fuel system + capacity check with calibrated barrel. 3mm cork to be fitted as specified.
5. Fit new Engine Pressure Sensor (Tony James)
6. Fit new Longines plug (Tony James)
7. Overhaul race Rear End and new CWP
8. Clean and drain drink system
9. Fit new fuel breakaways if available and when tested
10. Inspect Wing Pillars
11. Brake wear check - keep brakes for Monza practice
12. Fuel pump switch - change (Tony James)

Tailpiece

From a race engineer's or mechanic's point of view, there can be little doubt that in terms of technology, spectacle and raw power the 1985 and 1986 seasons were ones to savour. The following season saw the last of the turbo cars, already emasculated by the incorporation of mandatory pop-off valves to control boost. Many on the pit wall at Adelaide for the last qualifying session of 1986 knew they could expect something special.

'There's a transformation in the car when Senna "pulls the pin" and it is something to behold,' Steve Hallam recorded during that weekend. 'It's the turbo cars at their absolute peak for the very last time. We had one engine for one set of tyres, and another engine for the second set. The boys really wanted to do it because this was the ultimate in the indulgence of horsepower, the last qualifying lap for turbo engines of unlimited boost – one engine per lap. There was never going to be any more power in F1 than we had for that final qualifying in Adelaide 1986. We were at the end of a magnificent era.'

NO COLD STARTS

Due to the tight tolerances within the engine and turbochargers, the Renault turbo F1 engines could never be started 'from cold'.

A pre-warming system, using an external Kenlowe water heater and pump with quick-release couplings, was used to circulate warmed coolant through the respective systems for around one to two hours before running. This allowed the engine block, heads and ancillaries to reach sufficient temperature to expand, avoiding damage to piston rings, bearings and turbine blades as well as thermal shocks to the block and heads from excessively rapid temperature change from cold.

When the dashboard display indicated 60 degrees centigrade, the pre-heater could be removed and, with the ECU and spark box disconnected and spark plugs removed, the engine was 'spun' on the air starter until 2.0 bar oil pressure was seen on the gauge in the cockpit and the red oil-pressure warning light was extinguished. Once this had been achieved, the spark plugs were refitted, the ECU and spark box reconnected and the engine could be started.

Even when running, the tight tolerances required a steady warm-up process to bring the components to full operating temperature, with initial running at a steady 3,500rpm fast idle until a minimum of 70 degrees was indicated. At this stage the engine was to be lightly 'blipped' on the throttle past 6,000rpm, the minimum speed at which the alternator was activated. As temperatures stabilised, continued blipping to higher revs could then be initiated provided no undue load was put on the engine.

ABOVE Elio de Angelis and two Renault Sport engineers begin the engine-start cycle with a Lotus 97T. *(Classic Team Lotus)*

Chapter Six
The cars today

Today, three decades since the cars last raced, they have proven to be remarkable survivors. Eight cars in total were built: four examples of the Lotus 97T (driven by Senna and de Angelis in 1985) and four of the 98T (driven by Senna and Dumfries in 1986). Thanks to their iconic status, all eight survive, despite – or perhaps because of – the fact that they have never been eligible for any subsequent race series.

OPPOSITE Classic Team Lotus Works driver Andrew Beaumont prepares to demonstrate 97T/2 at the Goodwood Festival of Speed under the watchful eye of Chris Dinnage. *(Classic Team Lotus)*

RIGHT Ayrton Senna's first 97T, chassis 01, is now owned by Japanese racer Katsu Kubota. *(Classic Team Lotus)*

BELOW After restoration by Classic Team Lotus, 97T/1 was demonstrated at Suzuka in 2010 by Bruno Senna. *('Morio')*

BOTTOM Katsu Kubota's chassis 97T/1 prior to demonstration at Suzuka. *(Club Lotus Japan)*

The 1985 cars

Lotus 97T/1

Owned by Japanese collector and racing driver Katsu Kubota, the first car built, Lotus 97T/1, was driven by both Senna and de Angelis during the 1985 season before becoming the team's spare car.

Kubota has been a front-runner in historic events around the world since 2006, driving a collection of cars ranging from Group C sports cars to the ex-Ronnie Peterson Lotus 72, which, following restoration by Classic Team

Lotus, he races in Historic Grand Prix events across Europe. Classic Team Lotus worked with Kubota on the restoration of 97T/1, which culminated in 2010 in the car being demonstrated at Suzuka with Bruno Senna, Ayrton's nephew, reuniting the famous Senna helmet colours with the car.

Lotus 97T/2

Perhaps the most historically significant of the eight cars, 97T/2 was brand new when it was taken over by Ayrton Senna for the second race of the 1985 season, the Portuguese Grand Prix. This, of course, was the race in which Senna trounced all opposition on the rain-soaked track to take his maiden victory, a race that Ayrton himself regarded as his best-ever drive.

'Once I nearly spun in front of the pits, like Prost, and I was lucky to stay on the road,' said Senna. 'People think I made no mistakes, but that's not true – I've no idea how many times I went off! Once I had all four wheels on the grass, totally out of control, but the car came back on the circuit. Everyone said "fantastic car control". It was just luck.

'People later said that my win in the wet at Donington in '93 was my greatest performance

– no way – I had traction control! OK, I didn't make any real mistakes, but the car was so much easier to drive. It was a good win, sure, but, compared with Estoril '85, it was nothing, really.'

The car continued to be raced by Senna into the later stages of the 1985 season and, when superseded by the Lotus 98T, it remained at Team Lotus headquarters. When in 1995 Team Lotus International established the Classic activity, 97T/2 became one of the key cars in the collection and nowadays, run by Classic Team Lotus Works, it is demonstrated at events and tracks around the world.

ABOVE Chassis 97T/2 is perhaps the most historic of all as it was used by Ayrton Senna to score his maiden Formula 1 victory in the Portuguese Grand Prix at Estoril in 1985. *(Classic Team Lotus archive)*

RIGHT Chassis 97T/2 has remained in the hands of Team Lotus continuously and is today part of the Classic Team Lotus Works collection. *(Classic Team Lotus)*

ABOVE Classic Team Lotus personnel with the gas-turbine, four-wheel-drive Lotus 56. Bob Dance, at far right, was chief mechanic through the Senna era. *(Classic Team Lotus)*

ABOVE RIGHT Classic Team Lotus is directed by Clive Chapman, son of the Lotus founder. *(Ian Wagstaff)*

CLASSIC TEAM LOTUS

As a company, Classic Team Lotus is unique in the world of motorsport heritage. No other organisation can directly trace not only its heritage but also an unbroken line of experience, records and knowledge back to the original factory and also be run by the son of the company founder.

Colin Chapman's widow, Hazel, and son, Clive, are directors of a company that provides restoration, maintenance and operational support for owners of Lotus racing cars around the world. They are supported by many staff who worked on and around the cars when they were new: Bob Dance started with Lotus in 1960, worked with Graham Hill, Jochen Rindt and Emerson Fittipaldi, and was chief mechanic on the Lotus-Renault turbo cars of the Senna era; Chris Dinnage joined Team Lotus in 1982,

RIGHT Classic Team Lotus maintains, restores and races Lotus cars from every era. *(Ian Wagstaff)*

helped build the 95T, 97T and 98T cars for the team, and today is team manager of Classic Team Lotus; and Steve Allen, who has worked at Hethel since the days of the Lotus 72, looks after Classic Team Lotus's accounts.

The prime objectives of Classic Team Lotus are to preserve and promote the history of the team and act as a point of focus for all owners of the cars that established the Team Lotus legend. The fact that many of its staff originally designed, built or operated the cars is a massive bonus for customers. So, too, is an extensive archive of original drawings, components and reference materials: original parts lists, design drawings, engineers' records and photographs enable the exact specification of a component to be confirmed, and in addition Classic Team Lotus's own collection of cars provides reference points. The company is able to supply either an original spare with appropriate certification or a new part made to the original specification.

In addition to owning priceless racing cars in their own right, Classic Team Lotus is also the only Formula 1 World Championship-winning marque to establish a works team in historic motorsport.

'For those owners who believe their cars were built to be raced,' says Clive Chapman, 'Classic Team Lotus Works will organise everything from transport to race preparation at historic motorsport events.'

During 2014 and 2015, Classic Team Lotus raced cars in historic events as far afield as Singapore, Abu Dhabi, the United States and Mexico, acting both as a support event for modern Formula 1 races and as the stars of the show in their own right.

Chapman has also instigated the Classic Team Lotus Register, with the aim of identifying all the surviving single-seat, open-wheel racing cars and to make contact with their owners.

'There were 58 *monoposto* designs built by Team Lotus, from the Type 12 to the Type 102,' says Chapman. 'In total nearly 1,400 examples were built, of which nearly 550, including all eight of the Lotus 97T and 98T cars, are known to have survived.'

Lotus 97T/3

Given the interest of Japanese race fans in the life and legend of Ayrton Senna, particularly following his Honda-powered World Championship-winning years from 1988 to 1991, it is perhaps unsurprising that one of the Brazilian's earlier race-winning cars is a prized museum exhibit.

Chassis 97T/3 is displayed in a gallery devoted to Senna's life and racing in the Harada Collection at the Kawaguchiko Motor Museum on the outskirts of Tokyo. Created by automobile importer and exporter Nobuo Harada, the museum contains more than 100 vehicles as well as the world's largest collection of Japanese military aircraft from the Second World War.

Lotus 97T/4

The last Lotus 97T to be constructed resides in Switzerland in the collection of Fredy Kumschick. A race team owner, car restorer and Lotus Cars distributor, Kumschick describes himself as a long-time Lotus fanatic having bought his first example, a Mk1 Lotus Cortina, back in 1965.

Kumschick is equally passionate about Formula 1 and, as an admirer of Senna, he decided to try to acquire examples of the cars that the Brazilian drove. Ultimately he purchased three: 97T/4, a 98T and Honda-powered 99T.

'I bought the 97T at the end of the 1985 season, directly from Team Lotus, for next to

ABOVE Seen here in Canada in 1985, chassis 97T/3 now resides in the Kawaguchiko Motor Museum in Tokyo. *(John Townsend, F1 Pictures)*

RIGHT Cars from Fredy Kumschick's Swiss-based collection, which includes Lotus 97T/4, await departure for Imola in 2014. *(Fredy Kumschick Racing)*

RIGHT A full set: Fredy Kumschick's chassis 97T/4 alongside 98T/2 and his Lotus-Honda 99T. *(Fredy Kumschick Racing)*

BELOW No mere fair-weather racer. Fredy Kumschick laps Imola in the rain in 97T/4. *(Rafael Lopez)*

nothing,' says Kumschick. 'I have no idea how much it is worth today.'

After almost a quarter of a century of displaying the car as a static exhibit in his showroom and at exhibitions, Kumschick and his team began a five-year restoration that culminated in its return to the race track in 2014 at Imola, as part of the commemoration of Senna on the 20th anniversary of his death. Undaunted by heavy rain at the event, Kumschick demonstrated the car with impunity, pointing out that the conditions were appropriate given that both Senna's 1985 victories had been on a wet track. He also paid a personal tribute to Senna on each lap as he passed the site of the Brazilian's accident.

'Every time I passed the Tamburello I waved my hand to Ayrton. I tell him I like rain too.'

The 1986 cars

Lotus 98T/1

It is perhaps right and proper that the first of the ultimate Lotus-Renault Formula 1 cars should reside in Brazil. This car, which was used by Senna as his 'qualifying car' for the early part of the 1986 season, is maintained in running condition in the ownership of the Senna Foundation.

The prime role of the Senna Foundation, a non-profit organisation led by Ayrton's sister Viviane (mother of Bruno Senna), is to provide education and resources for under-privileged children and young people in Senna's native Brazil. Regular displays of the car provide both fund-raising opportunities for the Foundation

and keep the memory of the great Ayrton Senna alive in his native country.

Lotus 98T/2

The second Lotus 98T chassis to be built was raced throughout the 1986 season by Johnny Dumfries, with a best result of sixth place in the Australian Grand Prix at Adelaide. Since its retirement from racing it has maintained an international travelling history.

For many years the car was owned by the Tamiya Collection, established by the world-renowned Japanese model maker, which was a Team Lotus sponsor in the early 1990s. The car was subsequently part of the collection of Swiss Lotus enthusiast and racer Fredy Kumschick and was taken by him in 2014 to

ABOVE Chassis 98T/1, Senna's early-season qualifying and race car, is now with the Senna Foundation in Brazil. *(John Townsend, F1 Pictures)*

LEFT Seen in period with Johnny Dumfries at the wheel, chassis 98T/2 had a spell in Japan and now resides in Switzerland. *(John Townsend, F1 Pictures)*

Ayrton Senna's family created the *Instituto Ayrton Senna* – the Senna Foundation – within a few months of his death. Based in the Pinheiros district of São Paulo and run by Ayrton's sister, Viviane, the Senna Foundation exists to turn into reality a vision described by Ayrton before his tragic death. He expressed a goal of uniting Brazilian businesses, governments, schools, universities and other organisations to create greater opportunities for Brazilian children and youth.

At the centre of the Senna Foundation's activities is a campaign to raise the literacy level of children, particularly those living in poverty and unable to access more formal education in Brazil's fast-growing cities. In schools supported by the Senna Foundation, education follows a curriculum prepared by the Foundation using special textbooks.

'Despite his wealth,' said Viviane, 'Ayrton knew something had to be done to close this gap between rich and poor. He asked me to plan some organisation that would help children have a better future. This was two months

before Imola. I began to work on a structure – but we did not have the opportunity to talk again.

'One thing Ayrton wanted was to give a percentage of the proceeds of *Senninha* – his comic-book and cartoon character – to the project. When he had the accident, the family decided that we would give 100% of the royalties. We worked quickly: he spoke to me in March, the accident was in May, and by July we had established the Senna Foundation. Since that time it has been estimated that the Foundation has spent around £60 million, with the Senna family donating all the proceeds from the *Senninha* characters and the licensing of Ayrton's image to the charity.

Since its establishment, schools supported by the Senna Foundation have spread to approximately a quarter of Brazil's cities, giving over 17 million children an opportunity to receive education directly, and the Foundation has trained over 750,000 teachers. The three-times World Champion's legacy has saved millions of children from sliding into the oblivion of drugs, crime and life on the streets.

RIGHT Access to education and literacy for under-privileged young Brazilians is part of Senna's legacy. *(Instituto Ayrton Senna)*

BELOW The Senna Foundation fulfils Ayrton Senna's wish to provide support for under-privileged young Brazilians. *(Instituto Ayrton Senna)*

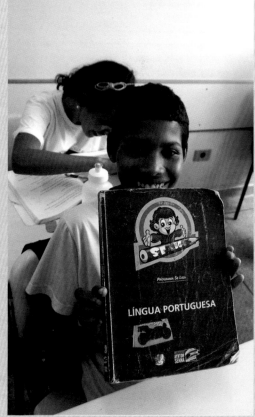

Imola, along with his Lotus 97T and 99T, for the Ayrton Senna 20th anniversary memorial event. The car has now passed to another owner who wishes to remain anonymous, but is thought to remain in Switzerland.

Lotus 98T/3

Chassis 98T/3, which was raced by Senna in the first eight grands prix of the 1986 season, including his two victories at Jerez in Spain and Detroit in the United States, is today one of the most active examples on the race track. It is owned and regularly demonstrated by Zak Brown.

Brown is a London-based American businessman and former professional racing driver. He founded Just Marketing International, the world's largest motorsport marketing agency, and, following its takeover by CSM Sport & Entertainment, subsequently became that agency's CEO. In 2009 Brown additionally formed, with business partner Richard Dean, the United Autosports racing team, which prepares modern racing sports cars such as the McLaren MP4-12C as well as historic cars, including those in Brown's own collection.

'Like so many, Senna was my hero,' Brown told journalist and fellow Lotus enthusiast Andrew Swift, 'so this car – and in that livery – it's so iconic, I just had to have it. I think it will prove to have good long-term investment potential, though I'd never sell it.'

Brown is committed to seeing cars driven. 'The previous owner had kept it hidden from the public eye, but I want the public to see it out. I tend only to drive it at safe circuits where I'm less likely to put it in the barriers. I recently drove a 2010 Lotus grand prix car and it was

a blast but almost disappointingly easy to drive. I know driving like Alonso isn't easy but in modern cars you can't over-rev them and you don't need to heel-and-toe. The 98T is completely manual and definitely takes more skill to drive quickly.'

ABOVE Zak Brown at speed at Goodwood in chassis 98T/3. *(Andrew Swift)*

LEFT Chassis 98T/3 proudly carries the period victory laurels of its two wins – a Team Lotus tradition. *(Author)*

BELOW A rare sight: the last two 98T chassis briefly shared workshop space in 2014. *(Author)*

Lotus 98T/4

The fourth and final Lotus 98T to be built was driven by Senna in 1986 from the ninth round at Brands Hatch until the 16th and final round in Australia.

Its most notable race was the 'wheel-banging' duel with the Williams of Nelson Piquet in the inaugural 1986 Hungarian Grand Prix, when, with ten laps remaining, the Lotus and Williams began swapping places for the lead, then 'leaning' on one another, then banging wheels – all at unabated speed. When the chequered flag was shown after two hours of racing, these were the only cars left on the lead lap.

This is also the 98T in which Senna scored the last two of his remarkable eight pole positions of 1986 – a fact that clearly confirms the final Lotus-Renault's status as the fastest car of its era.

Featured in most of the detail images in this manual, 98T/4 is today owned and demonstrated by DT Performance Engineering. Headed by Patrick Morgan, this Northamptonshire-based company has gained a worldwide reputation for maintaining historic racing cars to the highest levels of preparation and originality. They have carefully and sympathetically restored the car, determined to keep it in as original condition as possible.

RESTORATION CHALLENGES

The restoration of any historic racing car demands a no-compromises approach when it comes to every aspect of its engineering. The sheer performance of a classic Formula 1 car means that even a small failure can be catastrophic, and every owner of one of these iconic cars agrees that there are absolutely no short cuts when it comes to maintaining mechanical integrity and safety.

There are additional detail challenges too. It is perilously easy to over-restore such a car, producing an utterly immaculate example that does not reflect the true state of such a car when it was in the heat of competition. Lotus racing cars were never flawless, even when new. Like every team on the starting grid, Team Lotus presented tidy, clean, functional cars – tools for winning. The top restorers are determined to stay loyal to that philosophy.

One feature of the Lotus 97T and 98T is that every bolt on the chassis is unique: no two are the same length, each was originally cut to size individually, and each was originally copper-plated. A key, and lengthy, part of the restoration process requires the logging of where every individual bolt comes off the car so as to ensure that it goes back in exactly the same place. If a bolt is missing, the only solution is to buy a replacement, strip off its modern plating, cut it down and then copper-plate it again. It is a process that can take a whole week!

Even if original Speedline or Dymag wheels are available, common sense dictates that 30-year-old magnesium alloy, which is likely to have become porous and brittle, should not be trusted on a car that could theoretically still reach over 200mph. Fortunately, both wheel manufacturers are still in operation and retain the tooling to produce authentic modern replacements. Likewise, while some examples of original Goodyear Eagle tyres exist, they might not be safe at high speeds, so modern equivalents – including Avon speed hill-climb tyres – are used instead.

Another challenge is the fact that the Lotus-Renaults were born at the start of the computer age. The 98T was one of the very first cars to use microprocessor-driven ignition systems, which can cause more than a little

head-scratching. Organisations such as Classic Team Lotus and DT Performance have become expert in the analysis and reprogramming of race ECUs from this era, and they have even tracked down team laptops of the period and downloaded data from them.

It should also be remembered that 30 years ago even the idea of reprogramming a processor was still some way in the future. Instead, a single EPROM chip would be programmed for a specific set of characteristics; if you needed to change those characteristics, you had to replace the chip. Even Renault Sport Heritage, which still provides technical support for its engines of the time, has had to dig deep to find the people who programmed the EPROM chips originally.

ABOVE Patrick Morgan (right) and his team at DT Performance have gained an industry-wide reputation for their restorations. *(James Ward)*

BELOW Fastidious attention to detail is essential when restoring a 30-year-old Formula 1 car with enormous performance potential. *(Courtesy of Patrick Morgan)*

Epilogue

They remain the fastest Lotus cars ever built and can be ranked among the most powerful racing cars ever to take to a racing circuit. The Lotus 97T and 98T are icons for other reasons too. Their technical attainments – over 1,000bhp and the most advanced aerodynamics of the era – were combined with the swansong of the now legendary John Player Special livery and, of course, the connection with one of the greatest racing drivers of all time, the late, great Ayrton Senna.

This manual, therefore, is not just about a great racing car. It is also about an intense era of competition. The buttoned-down world of current Formula 1 simply does not offer a spectacle to equal that of three decades ago.

In many respects there are good reasons for this. The fact that two of the Lotus's contemporary drivers, Senna and Elio de Angelis, are no longer with us, having been killed in motor racing accidents in subsequent seasons, points to an era in which the risks

were greater, with both car and track safety less advanced than today.

There is no denying, though, that in this period Formula 1 was spectacular and the cars were simply awe-inspiring. Thanks to the passion of today's owners – Clive Chapman's Classic Team Lotus, Patrick Morgan, Fredy Kumschick and Zak Brown among others – we can still enjoy some of that spectacle at demonstrations today.

The drama of these cars has not diminished with time. Even today, the gruff bark of a 1980s turbo V6 is three times louder than a current Formula 1 engine and the sound has much more resonance.

Back in the 1980s, in full cry with no compromises, Formula 1 was going through a crazy period. The abiding comment from those who drove, worked on or even just saw these cars in their heyday still remains: 'Did we really do that?'

BELOW The Lotus 98T – synonymous with Ayrton Senna and the fastest Lotus ever built.
(James Ward)

Appendix 1

Lotus 98T specification

RIGHT, OPPOSITE AND OVERLEAF These three sheets show the original technical specification of the 98T as issued by Team Lotus on 2 February 1986.

John Player Special Team Lotus

WYMONDHAM, NORFOLK NR18 9RS, ENGLAND

TELEPHONE: NORWICH (0603) 811190
TELEX 975341
REGISTERED IN ENGLAND No. 1225833

CABLES: TEAM LOTUS, WYMONDHAM, NORFOLK
VAT REGISTRATION No. 283 4060 66

LOTUS TYPE 98T (JPS)

Powered by the latest version of the Renault Turbo V6 1500 Formula One engine, the JPS 98T represents a further logical development of the recent very successful family of Gerard Ducarouge designed cars which started with the JPS 95T in 1984 and continued with the JPS 97T which took eight pole positions and three Grand Prix victories in 1985.

The change in regulations limiting fuel capacity to 195 litres has allowed a smaller, stronger carbon fibre/aluminium honeycomb composite chassis to be produced and further refinements in both the front and rear suspension geometries are incorporated although pull rod suspension is retained.

A new six speed gearbox to make better use of the power characteristics of the more economical 1986 version of the Renault engine has been made at no increase in weight over the previous five speed unit.

The lower chassis height behind the driver's head has allowed the fuel management computer and "black box" recorder to be relocated there for easier access and reduced wiring complexity. A further computer gives the driver an instant read-out of his fuel status during the race.

Intercooling and oil/water radiators are similar to the earlier car but the one-piece body top now lifts off from the undertray line to allow the easiest possible access for the mechanics.

The aerodynamic package including deflectors and dynamic turbo air intakes remains very similar to the 1985 car but detail revisions are visible in brake ducting.

February 2 1986

Registered Office : KETTERINGHAM HALL, NORWICH, NORFOLK NR18 9RS
XXXXXXXXXXXXXXXXXXXXXXXXXXXXXXXXXXXXXXXXXXXXXX
Directors: F.R. BUSHELL, F.C.A., H.P. CHAPMAN, A.C. RUDD, B.Sc.Eng. P.E. WARR, P.G. WRIGHT, M.A.
WORLD CHAMPION CAR CONSTRUCTORS 1963, 1965, 1968, 1970, 1972, 1973, 1978.

JPS 98T TECHNICAL DESCRIPTION

MAIN DIMENSIONS	Overall length	422 cm
	Overall width	215 cm
	Weight	540 kg
	Wheelbase	272 cm
	Track	Front 181.6 cm
		Rear 162.0 cm

ENGINE   Renault V6 Turbo

CLUTCH   7.25" (18.4 cm) diameter twin plate Automotive Products hydraulically operated by an annular coaxial slave cylinder machined into the bell housing

GEARBOX   Six speed. Team Lotus designed and manufactured using some Hewland internals

WHEEL BEARINGS   Front - double row angular contact ball bearings
                   Rear - double row angular contact ball bearings

BRAKES   Front and rear - outboard single caliper Lotus/Brembo brakes operating on ventilated S.E.P. carbon discs. Driver adjustable brake balance.

WHEELS   Front - 13" diameter x 11½" wide
               Rear - 13" diameter x 16.3" wide

TYRES   Goodyear radials

FRONT SUSPENSION   Fabricated steel wishbones with pull rod operated inboard spring damper units and wide base lower wishbones. Fabricated steel uprights. Driver adjustable front anti-roll bar

REAR SUSPENSION   Fabricated steel rockers and wishbones with pull rod operated inboard spring damper unit. Fabricated steel uprights

DAMPERS   Gas/hydraulic supplied by Koni

CHASSIS   Carbon fibre/Kevlar skins with aluminium honeycomb monocoque, and Kevlar rope reinforcing

FUEL CELL   ATL single rubberised fabric cell located behind the driver within the main structure

BODYWORK	Kevlar one piece nose cockpit surround and tail. Carbon fibre flat underbody
WINGS	Carbon fibre, adjustable main elements and trim tabs front and rear
COOLING	Combined water/oil coolers and air/air intercoolers symmetrically mounted on either side of the chassis
LUBRICATION	The oil tank is incorporated within the bell housing between the engine and gearbox
LIFE SUPPORT SYSTEM	The car is fitted with fire extinguishers for the cockpit and engine bay and a helmet air supply system
ELECTRICS	As supplied by Renault

Appendix 2

Renault engine specification

Configuration	90-degree, V6, twin turbo
Capacity	1,492cc
Bore	86mm (EF4); 80.1mm (EF15)
Stroke	42.8mm (EF4); 49.4mm (EF15)
Compression ratio	7.0:1 to 7.5:1
Maximum rpm	11,000 (EF4); 13,000 (EF15C)
Firing order	1–6–3–5–2–4
Turbochargers	Two Garrett, up to 5.7 bar boost
Valve train	Four overhead camshafts, belt-driven, four valves per cylinder; pneumatically closed on EF15*bis* and EF15C
Ignition	Marelli ignition; Renix or Renault engine-management system
Fuel injection	Weber or Bosch; twin injectors per cylinder on EF15 engine
Weight	160kg (EF4); 154kg (EF15) – includes turbo system and clutch

Appendix 3

Race results

1985					
	Circuit	Number	Driver	Start position	Result
1	Brazil, Rio de Janeiro	11	Elio de Angelis	3	3
		12	Ayrton Senna	4	Electrical (3)
2	Portugal, Estoril	11	Elio de Angelis	4	4
		12	Ayrton Senna	1	1
3	San Marino, Imola	11	Elio de Angelis	3	1
		12	Ayrton Senna	1	7 (Out of fuel)
4	Monaco	11	Elio de Angelis	9	3
		12	Ayrton Senna	1	Engine (1)
5	Canada, Montréal	11	Elio de Angelis	1	5
		12	Ayrton Senna	2	16
6	United States, Detroit	11	Elio de Angelis	8	5
		12	Ayrton Senna	1	Accident (4)
7	France, Paul Ricard	11	Elio de Angelis	7	5
		12	Ayrton Senna	2	Accident/engine (15)
8	Britain, Silverstone	11	Elio de Angelis	8	Not classified (16)
		12	Ayrton Senna	4	10 (fuel/injection)
9	Germany, Nürburgring	11	Elio de Angelis	7	Engine (3)
		12	Ayrton Senna	5	Transmission (10)
10	Austria, Österreichring	11	Elio de Angelis	7	5
		12	Ayrton Senna	14	2
11	Netherlands, Zandvoort	11	Elio de Angelis	11	5
		12	Ayrton Senna	4	3
12	Italy, Monza	11	Elio de Angelis	6	6
		12	Ayrton Senna	1	3
13	Belgium, Spa-Francorchamps	11	Elio de Angelis	9	Turbo (16)
		12	Ayrton Senna	2	1
14	Europe, Brands Hatch	11	Elio de Angelis	9	5
		12	Ayrton Senna	1	2
15	South Africa, Kyalami	11	Elio de Angelis	6	Engine (4)
		12	Ayrton Senna	4	Engine (10)
16	Australia, Adelaide	11	Elio de Angelis	10	Black-flagged (5)
		12	Ayrton Senna	1	Engine (7)

1986					
	Circuit	Number	Driver	Start position	Result
1	Brazil, Rio de Janeiro	11	Johnny Dumfries	11	9
		12	Ayrton Senna	1	2
2	Spain, Jerez	11	Johnny Dumfries	10	Gearbox (6)
		12	Ayrton Senna	1	1
3	San Marino, Imola	11	Johnny Dumfries	17	Wheel bearing (21)
		12	Ayrton Senna	1	Wheel bearing (4)
4	Monaco	11	Johnny Dumfries	–	Did not qualify
		12	Ayrton Senna	3	3
5	Belgium, Spa-Francorchamps	11	Johnny Dumfries	13	Spun off (13)
		12	Ayrton Senna	4	2
6	Canada, Montréal	11	Johnny Dumfries	16	Accident (14)
		12	Ayrton Senna	2	5
7	United States, Detroit	11	Johnny Dumfries	14	7
		12	Ayrton Senna	1	1
8	France, Paul Ricard	11	Johnny Dumfries	12	Engine (10)
		12	Ayrton Senna	1	Accident (2)
9	Britain, Brand Hatch	11	Johnny Dumfries	10	7
		12	Ayrton Senna	3	Gearbox (15)
10	Germany, Hockenheim	11	Johnny Dumfries	12	Radiator (8)
		12	Ayrton Senna	3	2
11	Hungary, Hungaroring	11	Johnny Dumfries	8	5
		12	Ayrton Senna	1	2
12	Austria, Österreichring	11	Johnny Dumfries	15	Engine (22)
		12	Ayrton Senna	8	Engine (19)
13	Italy, Monza	11	Johnny Dumfries	17	Gearbox (9)
		12	Ayrton Senna	5	Transmission
14	Portugal, Estoril	11	Johnny Dumfries	15	9
		12	Ayrton Senna	1	4 (Out of fuel)
15	Mexico, Mexico City	11	Johnny Dumfries	17	Electrical (13)
		12	Ayrton Senna	1	3
16	Australia, Adelaide	11	Johnny Dumfries	14	6
		12	Ayrton Senna	3	Engine (6)

Appendix 4

Bibliography

Books

Autocourse (1985 & 1986), edited by Maurice Hamilton
Ayrton Senna: Driver, Hero, Legend, 'Autosport Legends' series
Ayrton Senna: The Team Lotus Years, Johnny Tipler
Lotus 49 Haynes Manual, Ian Wagstaff
Lotus 72 Haynes Manual, Ian Wagstaff
Team Lotus in Formula 1, Rainer Schlegelmilch and Hartmut Lehbrink
The 1000bhp Grand Prix Cars, Ian Bamsey
The Turbo Years: Grand Prix Racing's Battle for Power, Alan Henry

Magazines

Motor Sport, various articles by Nigel Roebuck, Simon Arron and Rob Widdows
Octane (May 2007), Lotus 98T article by Stephen Slater

Appendix 5

Useful contacts

Classic Team Lotus

Potash Lane, Hethel
Norfolk NR14 8EY
Tel 01953 601621
Website www.classicteamlotus.co.uk
Maintains, owns and races Team Lotus racing cars

DT Performance Ltd

Unit 12c Shackleton Hangar
Sywell Aerodrome
Northamptonshire NN6 0BN
Tel 01604 670345
Website www.dtperformanceltd.co.uk
Historic racing car restoration and preparation

United Autosports

Unit 1, Helios 47
Isabella Road
Leeds LS25 2DY
Tel 0845 4599959
Website www.unitedautosports.com
Racing car preparation and racing team

Kumschick Racing

Luzernerstrasse 57
6247 Schötz, Luzern
Tel (41) 41 980 05 80
Website www.kumschickracing.ch
Lotus garage and historic racing car preparation

Renault Sport Technologies

1/15 Avenue du President Kennedy
91177 Viry-Châtillon CEDEX
France
Tel (33) 1 69 12 58 00
Website www.renaultsport.com
Engine and technology supplier

Kawaguchiko Motor Museum

Narusawa-Mura, Fujizakura Kogen Nai
Minamitsuru-Gun, Yamanashi Prefecture
401-0320 Japan
Tel (81) 555 86 3511
Website www.car-airmuseum.com
Museum including Harada Collection and ex-Senna Lotus 97T

Index